OH, THE

Helga Tucque

Copyright Helga Tucque
All rights reserved

First edition printed: 2013

ISBN 978-0-9866407-3-5

To Andre

Index	Page #
1. THE DECISION	5
2. GETTING READY	8
3. GOODBYE GERMANY	12
4. THE SEA VOYAGE	15
5. JOURNEY ACROSS CANADA	19
6. EDMONTON	28
7. A NEW BEGINNING	32
8. SURPRISES	40
9. LEARNING THE ROPES	44
10. MISSED OPPORTUNITY	47
11. THE STRANGER	52
12. ANDRE	60
13. RUDE AWAKENING	63
14. MOVING AGAIN	65
15. THE WILDCAT	70
16. BONZO	73
17. THE ADVENTURE ROAD	77
18. THE RED SHOES	94
19. BUYING A HOUSE	98
20. THE SKI TRIP	101
21. MOTHER'S VISIT	113
22. THE EASTER WEEKEND	119
23. ROCK LAKE	129
24. KEYS	135
25. THE LAST WORD	138

1. THE DECISION

"I've sent in my application to the Canadian government. I'm going to emigrate. Who wants to come along?" Beaming with excitement my brother, Wilfried, called out, as he entered our tiny apartment. He frequently dropped in for a visit. At age twenty and single he was eager to see the world and explore new realms. After recently obtaining his cabinet-maker journeyman papers there was no reason to stay in Germany any longer.

"I'll go with you," I blurted out.

"And where do you want to get the money for the passage?" My husband, Kurt, asked, looking at me. He probably questioned my sanity for deciding such an important step on the spur of a moment. We had talked about the possibility of emigrating before, but Kurt had been dragging his feet. He had a steady job as a cabinet maker and no reason for leaving the country, but I was eager to find a better future. I was not happy in West Germany. The City of Wuppertal, where we lived at that time, was alien to me. I had no real friends here and all my relatives lived far away, except for Wilfried. If he was gone, there would be a void. He would be sorely missed.

Until recently Kurt and I, and a year later with our son, Andre, were living in one single room in the attic on the fourth floor without running water. It had to be fetched one and a half stories down at the toilet, which we shared with three other families. Fourteen families resided in that building. Every three weeks we were allowed one day for doing the laundry. The so-

5

called wash kitchen was in the basement. Everything was done by hand because there was no washing machine. On laundry day Andre, who was a toddler at that time, had to accompany me to the wash kitchen, as I had no one to look after him. Of course, he became soaking wet on numerous occasions trying to help, and I had to run the four flights upstairs to change his outfit. We finally had found that tiny apartment at the outskirts of Wuppertal for which we had to pay a substantial amount of money, 2,000 marks to be exact, as a loan for having the privilege of renting the apartment. I had received this money for having lost our home. It was paid by the German government to help people, who had lost their homeland, to get a new start. The apartment consisted of two rooms, and a sliver of a kitchen; the toilet was downstairs and had to be shared with the landlord and his family. This was a brand new house, but for lack of the owner's money some work was not yet completed. Our landlady used every opportunity to ask Kurt for favours finishing jobs or re-doing work that needed to be done properly. It was so easy and convenient having a cabinet maker in the house, one she did not have to pay. The housing shortage at that time was grave. People did almost anything just to have a place to stay. Some still lived in the former underground bunkers without daylight. Wuppertal had been severely bombed during WWII. But there were other reasons why I didn't want to stay in Germany. The progress we made achieving a lifestyle similar to what I had been used to before the war, was very slow. I missed many conveniences, which I had taken for granted when I was a child, like a washroom with a bathtub. It seemed as if I would never reach that goal while remaining in the ruins of Germany. Hope of ever returning home to Silesia had also vanished completely. Homesickness was not as acute as it had been in the beginning, but now there was the realization that we would most likely never return. What did we have to lose here? At one time we had considered emigrating to Australia or South America, but always put off making a decision.

Wilfried's proposal was the catalyst. Canada was the only country currently accepting immigrants. The U.S.A. had closed its doors for immigration of people who had no sponsors, and we certainly did not qualify. If we wanted to go ahead with our plan, it had to be now, because Andre needed to start school next year. He would have to learn English to compete with the rest of the class.

"Oh, we'll sell everything we have and maybe the Canadian Government will lend us some money for the rest of the passage," I replied confidently.

"Well, if you will be able to accomplish all that, I'll go along," Kurt laughed. He doubted that I would have the stamina and patience to manage all the paperwork, sell our few belongings and whatever needed to be done. He had underestimated my desire and determination. I immediately wrote to the Canadian consulate asking for the application forms. They arrived in the mail a short time later together with brochures about life in Canada, her laws, and what to expect. Included were photos of single dwellings owned by German immigrants residing in the city of Edmonton, Alberta. They looked lovely with flower gardens in front. I had no clue where that city or province was located, or if there was work for Kurt, but what did I care? If we didn't like it there, we could move to another place. We were still young and healthy. There had been so much moving during my life already that one more time made no difference. I was used to leaving places and starting anew. These houses looked mighty tempting. Yes, that's what I wanted to have, a house of our own with roses growing in the front yard.

2. GETTING READY

Soon after returning the completed forms, we received an invitation to visit the Canadian consulate in Cologne. Kurt asked for a day off work so we could all go. Slowly the reality of having taken the first step began to sink in. It was a serious step, one that had far-reaching consequences. We realized that after leaving the country it would be a long time, if ever, until we would visit our relatives again. Air travel for ordinary people was still a dream of the future. Most ships needed at least ten days to cross the ocean.

It was only a short train ride to Cologne. The consulate was centrally located and we had no problem finding it. We sat in the visitor's room eagerly waiting for our turn to be ushered into the office. Finally the door opened, and we were asked to enter.

"Where would you like to live in Canada?" the friendly Canadian official asked during the interview.

"Edmonton," I replied promptly. The official gave me a strange look. I had the impression that he thought 'you must be a bit naive', but then he smiled. "That is a good place. I'm sure you'll like it there."

Alberta's economy was mostly agriculture at that time and Edmonton, the capital, a "hick" town. Although oil had been discovered a few years earlier, only a few people expected then that this part of the country would be teeming with new activity soon, and Alberta become one of the richest provinces in Canada. We had picked the right place without knowing it.

The official wrote down a few more details asking questions and stamping papers. Then he stood up extending his hand and shaking ours. "Everything seems to be in order. Goodbye and good luck. You'll soon hear from us," he said with that strange smile again. He may have felt sorry for us in his assumption that we were traveling to a wilderness area where foxes and wolves said goodnight to each other. It is possible that he was from Toronto or Montreal, where people still considered Alberta part of the Wild West. Maybe he wasn't so wrong at the time, but changes were already on the way.

After leaving the consulate we decided to visit Cologne cathedral, which was in walking distance from the consulate. We would probably never get a second chance to see this world famous landmark.

The cathedral is an impressive structure standing at about the centre of the old city. Construction of the building was started in the year 1248, but not fully completed until the 19th century. The original architect and builder had fallen to his death before finishing his work. Superstitious people of that time believed that he had been in cahoots with the devil, for the structure is so enormous and beautiful that no man would be capable of planning and constructing such a magnificent building without His help. The builder's fall to his death was considered his punishment for giving his soul to the evil one.

During WWII the cathedral was bombed repeatedly despite its high towers being visible from afar, but the sturdy stone walls withstood the onslaught. The damage was repaired after the war. Today the cathedral stands in its former glory, and poses a commanding presence. It is the most visited cathedral in Germany.

Entering the huge nave with the immensely high ceiling made me feel insignificant, like a kernel of sand in a vast ocean. Only a few tourists were visiting that early in the day. The silence was overpowering. We quietly walked along the centre to the other end admiring the stained glass windows, and whispering in awe. In my mind I pictured the numerous events that had taken place within these sturdy walls during the hundreds of years of their existence. Processions and festivities with all their glitter and pomp floated like a movie scene through my imagination. Kings were crowned here, royal babies baptised and Christmas and Easter celebrated. The population of Cologne may have gathered here to pray for deliverance when war was upon them or to celebrate victory.

A few weeks after the interview we received confirmation that our request had been granted.

Wilfried's papers arrived in the mail a week later despite his earlier application. He would have to take the next ship to Canada. Passage was booked immediately and the real work began. Getting rid of the few belongings was no problem. At that time people still needed things, but money was in short supply. Finally I found a couple who bought the lease for the small apartment complete with all its contents. We were only allowed a certain amount of luggage on our journey, so we had to plan very carefully what to take. Kurt's tools were rather heavy, but he was of the opinion that he might need them at Canada. It turned out not to be the case, but we didn't know it then. We therefore had to leave some of the things we desperately wanted and needed, like blankets and dishes in Germany.

"I'll ride the Vespa to Bremerhaven," Kurt announced a few days before our departure.

"Why do you want to do that?" I asked surprised.

"It'll only cost the price of gas to drive there. It is less than the train ticket. I can save a few marks. In Bremerhaven I'll find a buyer," he explained. "You and Andre can take the train."

I'm sure that the reason for this decision was his desire to ride the Vespa and not so much saving the money. Kurt's Vespa was a type of cheap motorcycle, which was in style at that time. He loved this means of transportation, as it came close to owning a car. I was not too happy about his decision of riding it such a long way. It was about a five-hour drive to the coast. Anything could happen on the way to Bremerhaven. What if he had an accident and was killed or severely injured? Would I have to leave with Andre or stay with my parents? Having sold everything already there was no turning back anymore. Oh, it would be most inconvenient if a mishap occurred. Numerous possibilities raced through my brain. What if!

3. GOODBYE GERMANY

It was the day before our departure when Kurt entered the apartment. He was bleeding profusely from his nose, his jacket was torn, his face dirty, and one sleeve hung loosely on a few threads.

"What on earth happened to you?" I cried out shocked, seeing him standing at the door in such a deplorable condition.

"I've had an accident," he admitted downheartedly, wiping the blood from his nose. "The Vespa is a wreck."

"How did that happen?" I enquired.

He explained to me that he had hit a rock lying on the road. It had thrown him off balance and sent him flying through the air. He had landed in the middle of the road. Luckily at that moment there hadn't been another vehicle driving close behind him. It could have been much worse. The Vespa was a write-off. Kurt's nose was blue and swollen for a while, but otherwise he was not seriously injured. Now we would all have to take the train to Bremerhaven, which was fine with me.

We all met at my parent's home in Bremerhaven for our goodbye party. Kurt and I were married in that city. We had both lived in Bremerhaven during the year prior to our marriage. My sister Erika with her husband came from Hamburg. Wilfried arrived also. It would be the last time the entire family would be together. There were also aunts, uncles and cousins, who had moved to this city several years earlier. They all came to see us off.

From left to right: Father, Mother, Wilfried, Reinhard, Helga, Kurt, Erika.

From my parents' windows on the third floor of an apartment building, we had watched on numerous occasions boats leave the Columbuskaje for different destinations. There were ships loaded with American soldiers returning to their homeland, emigrant boats and luxury liners. They always started their journey at midnight. The cabins were all lit, their lights mirroring on the water's surface. Then we heard a faint blast and slowly the ship moved out to sea. With lights fading in the mist, the big boats disappeared into the darkness of night. Then the harbour became quiet again. It was always a spectacular light show, and worth the effort of staying up late. Now it would be our turn to be on one of these ocean liners.

The last day was spent visiting friends and doing last minute shopping. At boarding time, the entire family accompanied us to the harbour. Our hearts were heavy. It must have been especially painful for my parents losing two of their children within one week. Our father understood our decision, as he himself had left the country when he was a young man, but had returned to Germany to save his parent's business. He had tried to leave again after the war, but because of his age and the state of his health did not get permission. Kurt was unable to say goodbye to his parents, as they lived in East Germany and were not allowed to leave that so-called Communist paradise. He would never see any of them again.

There were the last embraces with tears rolling down our cheeks as we walked up the steps to the deck to find our cabin, which was located in the bow, where the movement at sea was most noticeable. Kurt was accustomed to being on a ship, having served with the marines during the war. He never was seasick, but it was the first sea voyage for Andre and me. We were a little apprehensive not knowing what to expect.

Then we stood at the bulwark waving our last goodbye to the family. Memories raced through my mind. I had to think of the time when we had to leave our home in Silesia, a place I had loved so much. At that time we had no idea where destiny would take us. Our future looked uncertain, bleak and hopeless. Now we were full of anticipation of the new life that awaited us in that far away land across the ocean. Would we be welcome there? Would we find the life we were looking for: prosperity, wealth, and most important of all peace? It was an emotional time saying goodbye to our country of birth. That land had caused so much suffering and hardship, yet we were a part of it.

The heavy ship started to move ever so slightly. Then there was a blast from the bridge, and we were on our way. The city lights grew faint in the distance. We waved one more time then slowly walked to our cabin.

4. THE SEA VOYAGE

Bremerhaven is situated at the mouth of the river Weser, a distance away from the open water of the North Sea. During the night we reached the ocean. The waves were getting rougher. A strong wind was blowing from the west. After a fitful sleep breakfast didn't taste so good. Stomachs began to churn. Some people were already hanging over the bulwark with green faces. A friend of the family, who worked as a radio operator on this ship, the "Arosa Kulm", a converted freighter, had told us that the captain was seasick for the first three days of each journey. Imagine, the captain being seasick! Andre looked very pale. He didn't want to eat anything and told me that he didn't feel good.

"I would better take him to the cabin and put him to bed," I said to Kurt.

At about noon the outline of a white coastline came into view. The heavy ship had stopped her engines. It was quiet. An announcement came over the loudspeaker that this was the Isle of Wight in England. We were taking on more passengers. The harbour at the island was not suitable for a large ship like the *Arosa Kulm*, so passengers had to be brought in small boats. We went up to the deck, and stood at the bulwark watching the new passengers come aboard. They all originated in Finland and were also destined for Canada. It was not possible to communicate with them as they spoke Finnish, a language difficult to understand. Very few spoke English, but the group kept to themselves.

The farther we traveled out to the Atlantic, the higher the waves were rolling. Then it started to rain. Heavy drops hit the porthole and visibility was impaired. The wind became stronger whipping the waves until white crowns formed.

Andre was seasick. Listless he lay in bed. I stayed with him in the cabin. The strain of getting ready for the journey had taken its toll on me too. I was dead tired, but fortunately did not have to throw up. At one point the ship's doctor came to the cabin to check if we were coping with sea sickness. During most of the sea voyage I stayed in the cabin lying on my bed or caring for Andre.

Kurt entered the cabin one day shouting excitedly: "Come quick, look out of the window." He spent all day on deck or attended inside activities when it rained too much. The dining room was almost empty during the roughest days, so he could eat to his heart's content. For him it was a pleasurable journey.

I stood up and groggily walked to the porthole. A huge ocean liner, the *Queen Mary*, sailed beside our ship. I guessed she was only three hundred metres away. Of course I could be wrong in judging the distance. She was travelling so fast that it looked like a car passing on a highway. After about half an hour she had completely disappeared on the horizon.

We had been at sea for nine days already. Time passed very slowly. All we wished for was having solid ground under our feet again. Finally the weather cleared and blue sky stretched above. Most of the passengers came to the deck and stood at the bulwark, having survived sea sickness. Gigantic icebergs, like the one that sank the Titanic, glistened in the bright sunlight as they slowly drifted south. Against the back drop of an ink blue sky they made for an impressive sight. Then a grey rock seemed to grow out of the murky water.

"This is the coast of Newfoundland," the captain announced.

Andre

A few hours later the boat entered the St. Lawrence Seaway. The water became much calmer. Andre was able to come on deck. His seasickness had finally subsided. The countryside on both banks looked inviting. We saw houses and farms with white and black cows grazing on the rich lush greens. Cars drove along a road. The mood of the passengers improved considerably. Green faces gave way to healthy colours, and laughter was heard again.

"That looks very nice," Kurt commented admiring the countryside. "If we don't like it in Edmonton we'll come back and settle here."

A castle loomed high up on an incline with numerous little turrets. Its countless windows were gleaming like gold in the evening sunlight. We later learned that this was hotel Chateau Frontenac. Beneath the chateau a city began to emerge, the City of Quebec.

As we approached Quebec harbour, the *Queen Mary* passed us again sailing in the opposite direction on her way to the next destination. Anchored in the harbour was an array of cargo ships flying flags of many different colours and designs, the same as in Bremerhaven. Sounds of foreign languages drifted over. We had arrived in Canada, the land of opportunity and hope for a new life.

5. JOURNEY ACROSS CANADA

The next morning, after completion of all paperwork, we were allowed to step on Canadian soil. It felt awkward walking on solid ground again like losing one's balance. We wobbled along, swaying from one side to the other until we found our bearings. The official at the harbour office told us that a train was waiting on the rails to take all immigrants to Montreal at about noon. We had lots of time.

"What are we going to do in the meantime?" I asked.

"Let's look around." Kurt suggested. "We should buy some food for the trip. It probably costs a fortune in the dining car. We mustn't use too much of the money we brought along. We'll need it later. Maybe we'll find a grocery store, where we can get a few things."

We had been told that it would be a very long journey lasting three days and nights. I had experienced a long journey before. It had taken us that much time to get from Silesia to West Germany when we were deported after the war; the only difference was the distance had been a tiny fraction of the one we were facing now. Because of our limited money reserves, we had bought ordinary train tickets and would have to sleep sitting upright on our seats in the compartment during the night. On the train to West Germany we had slept on the wooden floor of a box car unable to stretch our legs. There had not been enough room for so many people. We thought that sitting on upholstered seats would not pose a problem. Andre would be small enough to lie down. How wrong we were! We soon discovered that sitting up all night was very uncomfortable.

Walking up the hill we found a little shop selling groceries. The elderly couple inside, who seemed to own the place, did not pay much attention to us. They pretended not to speak or understand any English or German. Even with the limited French vocabulary, Kurt had learned during the war, we made no progress. What should we do? In Germany it was not allowed to take things from the shelves, but the couple's behaviour didn't leave us much choice.

"I guess we'll have to help ourselves," I finally said. We viewed the display of food items. There were cans with vegetables and various soups, but these items were useless, as we had nothing to heat them with. We needed bread, but there was no brown bread anywhere. The only bread, as far as we could see, was snow-white.

"They probably don't sell rye bread here. We'll have to make do with that." Kurt grabbed one loaf and a few bananas, a pound of butter and three large bottles of orange juice. We didn't find any deli sausage. Perhaps they didn't sell any.

"This will have to do," he said and paid the store owners.

Arriving in Montreal in the late afternoon we were told that a bus was waiting outside the station to take us to a different train station. Together with all the other immigrants, who had been on the same ship, we made our way to the bus. The driver must have been in great hurry. He most likely was late meeting his schedule. He took off before we were all seated. Some people were holding onto the bars for dear life swaying back and forth until they were able to reach a seat. The traffic was *"furious"*, but it didn't seem to deter the driver from racing through the crowded streets. With great skill he maneuvered the heavy bus among the chaos of vehicles. Not being used to such speed we all prayed for our lives. *That was a close call! Panic! Screeching brakes! Almost hit! Loud honking!* How the driver managed to get us to the station without smashing up the vehicle seemed like a miracle. Finally we reached the main railway station, unhurt. The bus came to an abrupt halt. Everyone gave out a sigh of relief.

The transcontinental train to Vancouver was waiting on the rails. After finding our designated seats we stowed away our hand luggage. We had been told the rest would be delivered upon our arrival in Edmonton. We felt a bit uncertain about that arrangement, because when travelling on a train in Germany, every person had to look after his or her own luggage. All seats in this compartment were occupied by immigrants.

It was the middle of August, and the days were noticeably getting shorter. Daylight was fading more quickly. Late in the evening the heavy engine slowly started to roll out of the station. Our first day on Canadian soil came to an end.

We had been travelling for about an hour or so when suddenly there was a jolt and the sound of screeching brakes, and then the train came to a sudden stop.

"What's the matter?" "Has there been an accident?" "Did the train come off the rails?" "Why are we stopping?" everyone asked, looking around. We could see the train personnel outside holding up lamps and examining the wheels. They were discussing things. Then a furious conductor entered the compartment.

"Who pulled the emergency brake?" he yelled, but no one answered. Most of the occupants could not understand what he was saying. I translated as well as my limited vocabulary allowed. I had taken English lessons in high school, and later worked a few months for an American family in Bremerhaven, but was by no means fluent in this language.

"If that happens again the person responsible will be taken into custody," the angry conductor threatened. Some young guys at the other end snickered. They stood together in the corner whispering. It probably was one of those teenagers who had pulled that prank. They seemed very proud of themselves after the conductor left the compartment, laughing as if they had accomplished an heroic act.

During the night we arrived in Toronto. A loudspeaker announced the name. The city was bathed in blazing lights. Neon signs on stores, cars driving everywhere and despite the late hour still fairly heavy traffic. It was a strange sight seeing so many lights and no ruins like in all large cities in Germany at that time. It looked like a vibrant place.

"This must be a very large city," Kurt declared. Andre had fallen asleep in my lap. The compartment almost emptied here as most of the German immigrants left, having chosen Toronto as their destination. A few Canadian passengers boarded. We had plenty of room to sit comfortably from thereon. Andre was able to

23

stretch out completely on two seats. It was a blessing, as he was in desperate need of rest.

Hour after hour the train rattled through forests and along seemingly never-ending lakes. Despite the upholstered seats it was not easy to fall asleep. We dozed off and on. Then night turned into day again.

"I have a job already. The people are coming to pick me up," one of the German immigrants in the compartment boasted. With a flare of confidence he looked at us with pity, as if certain that he had made the right decision by signing up to work for a year. "I'm going to work on a farm." On and on he bragged how smart he had been to find a job before coming to Canada. He would not have to look for work or a place to stay.

It wasn't long after that speech that the conductor entered the compartment.

"You'll have to get off the train at the next stop," he advised the man showing him with his hand. At first the fellow didn't seem to understand, but then he nodded. His face betrayed his sudden apprehension. There was nothing but forest out there as far as the eye could see. No town or farm was anywhere in sight. About fifteen minutes later the train stopped in the middle of nowhere. There was not even a station house for shelter. The young man was lucky that the weather was pleasant, so waiting outside wouldn't pose a

24

problem. We all stood at the windows watching as he slowly descended. Forlornly he looked around. The bedraggled expression on his face spoke volumes. He seemed to be completely alone in this wilderness. There was no one waiting for him. We felt sorry for the poor fellow in his predicament. What would happen to him if he was not picked up? Were there wild animals lurking in the underbrush? What would he do when darkness fell? It also made us think of what awaited us upon our arrival in Edmonton. We didn't know a single soul there or anywhere else in Canada. Would we feel lost like this young man? Had we been too confident in assuming that everything would work out all right? Where was that city of Edmonton? Would people be hostile toward us? After all, the end of the war was not so long ago.

Hour after hour passed, then day turned to night again. We tried to sleep, but it was not easy sitting upright. It was not possible for an adult to stretch out completely, even on two seats. Andre was not eating properly. He didn't like the white bread or the orange juice, the butter was too salty, and all he ate was bananas. Was that journey ever going to end? Another day dawned. As far as the eye could see there was nothing but wheat fields now, miles and miles of yellow swaying stalks. It reminded one of waves in a vast ocean.

At noon the train stopped in Winnipeg, the capital of Manitoba. The conductor came to the compartment to tell us that we had an hour's wait. Our

25

provisions were eaten up and we all rushed out looking for a grocery store. Perhaps we would find some brown bread here. It felt good running and stretching our legs after sitting for so many hours.

"Do you have any rye bread?" I asked the lady at the counter upon entering a store not too far away from the train station.

"Sorry, no, we don't. We only sell white bread," she replied. We were disappointed, but at least I was able to communicate with her. She was helpful and friendly showing me where everything was. Our purchase consisted again for the most part of bananas. Bananas were easy to eat. Many items were useless as we only had a little pocket-knife but no plate. With the brown paper shopping bag we made our way back to the waiting train. We had hardly entered when the engine started to move. At first we thought that the train had to change rails or whatever else was needed, but it gathered speed and kept on going. Most of the other immigrants in our compartment had not yet returned. We looked at each other.

"What is going on? I thought we had an hour's wait. Did you misunderstand the conductor?" Kurt asked.

"No, I'm sure he said an hour," I replied. "I'm glad we returned right away."

At that moment the conductor entered the compartment.

"There are a number of people missing. You told us that the train had an hour's wait. What is going to happen to them? Their luggage and coats are still here," I told him.

That had his attention, but there was nothing he could do about it now. "I'll phone the next station and let them know," he finally said.

We worried, wondering how these people would manage. "I hope they carry some money," Kurt commented.

"They probably do, because they went shopping. They may have to stay in a hotel overnight and get on the train tomorrow," I said. "But it'll be costly."

After about half an hour the train stopped at a small station. We didn't trust our eyes. All of the missing people from the compartment stood at the platform waiting. Amazing! How was that possible? There was a big "hello".

"How did you manage to get here so fast?" we asked after they boarded.

"When we saw the train leave without us, we collected all our money. It was enough to rent a taxi. We told the driver to get us to the next station as fast as he could drive. He sure did. We were hanging under the ceiling more than we sat on our seats. He drove like the devil himself. The vehicle was so crowded that we sat on top of each other. It was a drive I won't ever forget," one of the immigrants related.

The last of our fellow immigrants had left the train in Saskatchewan. We were the only ones left bound for Edmonton. It was early morning, a brilliant morning, one of those rare summer mornings when a blue sky stretched above and the air smelled of ripening wheat and clover.

"The next stop is Edmonton," the conductor called out, opening the door to the compartment. Now it won't be long until we were to see our new home town. My heart started to beat faster. I hadn't been afraid until now, but suddenly I was scared, really scared. What awaited us in that foreign city? Had I made the right decision in choosing this place? Would we run into insurmountable problems? So many thoughts raced through my brain. Andre was sick again. He lay on the seat, pale and unresponsive. The journey had taken its toll on him. It was high time that he got off that train and on solid ground.

Today was our 6th wedding anniversary. Kurt and I stood at the window watching the countryside swoosh by. Ripening wheat fields, rolling hills and then lush grass with cattle grazing, a picture of peace. It reminded me of the landscape in southern Sweden, where I had visited my relatives several years before. Then we reached the outskirts of the city. Finally our long journey came to an end.

6. EDMONTON

The train rolled into the station coming to a halt. It looked like a station in any European city, except for the absence of other trains. "Edmonton," a voice called over the loudspeaker.

We gathered our hand luggage and stepped down onto the platform. Very few people left the train here. They quickly disappeared. We were slowly walking along the platform, uncertain as to what to do next, when suddenly we heard a voice calling our name. That was strange. How was it possible that anyone knew our name? It certainly wasn't a common name.

"Welcome to Edmonton," a smiling young man called out in German as he approached, extending his hand to greet us. At that moment I was certain that everything would turn out all right. It was a warm, pleasant and completely unexpected welcome, blowing away all our fears and apprehensions. I had to think of our arrival in the little village in West Germany so many years ago in 1946. Nobody wanted us then. We were deportees, homeless people with nothing but our clothes on our backs. For three hours the mayor of this village had quarreled with our future landlord. They were shouting and cursing.

"Why don't you send them back to where they came from?" The man had yelled furiously. "I don't have any room for them, and I don't want a family of six."

In my mind I can still hear his angry shouts. It had been so degrading to be deported after losing everything and then being rejected by our own countrymen. "Welcome to Edmonton," these three words sounded so comforting, so friendly. They made all the difference. I fell in love with this city

29

immediately, a love that never wavered for more than fifty years.

"I'm from the Canadian immigration office," the young man introduced himself. "Please follow me. Our office is across the street from the railway station. I must check your papers, but that will only take a few minutes and then I'll call a taxi to take you to a hotel. You are probably very tired."

We sure were. Since being on solid ground again, Andre slowly began to perk up, but it was obvious that he was in need of sleep. Kurt lifted him up and carried him. The gentleman led us across the rails. Walking over rails would never be allowed in any large German city, because trains are running every few minutes. The young man explained that there was no danger as only one passenger train was running each day, the one we had just left.

After the formalities completed, a taxi arrived to drive us to the Kensington hotel. To our great surprise the driver also spoke German, but with a Bavarian dialect. This dialect is not easily understood by Germans from another area. Sometimes he had to repeat his words, because we didn't understand. We asked the young man where he came from. To our surprise he replied, "I was born in Edmonton. After the war I was stationed in Bavaria. That's where I picked up the language."

It was only a short distance to the hotel. After registration at the desk we were led to a comfortable room with a double bed. What a great feeling that was, to find a real bed with white linen sheets. Dead tired we dropped onto it falling asleep immediately. It was late afternoon when we awoke.

After the long journey without any conveniences we savored every moment under the hot shower. Clean and refreshed with teeth brushed we finally felt human again. Andre had recovered from his ordeal and was jumping around.

"I'm hungry," Kurt said. "Let's go and eat."

The official at the immigration office had supplied us with coupons for a meal at a restaurant on Jasper Avenue. I went to the hotel desk and inquired where we would find that place. "You can't miss it," the clerk explained. "Go east along Jasper Avenue. It's on your right."

It was Sunday afternoon. Jasper Avenue was deserted. All stores were closed. Very few cars were driving by and only a handful of pedestrians walked leisurely on the sidewalk looking at the display in the show windows. A car dealership had little coloured flags hanging on strings over their lot, but it was also closed. That was a strange and unfamiliar sight. It reminded me of a carnival or exhibition with its array of colours. At that time Premier Manning ruled this province with an iron fist. He was also a preacher, and did not allow any open business or pleasure activities on Sundays, not even sports events. The only gathering permitted was for church services. Drinking rules were very strict. Women were not allowed in beer parlours and only in a few places were husbands and wives allowed to drink a glass of beer together. Everyone had to sign and record their name and address at the government liquor store when buying a bottle of alcohol for home use.

We strolled along looking at the displays in the show windows. There was the *Hudson's Bay Company* with its history engraved on one of the outside walls. We passed the *Royal Bank* building and then there was the restaurant. Believe me, after three days eating mostly bananas and 'rubber bread' the meal tasted like it was made in the finest hotel kitchen.

7. A NEW BEGINNING

Life started in earnest the next morning. We were on our own now, having to overcome all the hurdles and obstacles, which may occur during a new beginning. The most urgent task was to find accommodation, because the cost for the hotel and eating in a restaurant were added to our outstanding debt with the Canadian government. Sooner or later we would have to pay back the money we owed. It was therefore imperative to find a place as soon as possible where we could cook our own meals and wash clothes soiled during the long journey. We also needed an address for the delivery of our remaining luggage.

Near the hotel entrance I discovered a stand with newspapers and purchased one copy. With the paper in hand I went back to our hotel room to study the ads for rental suites. To our dismay we discovered that rents were much higher here than in the old country or so it seemed. Many ads also specified that children were not wanted. That limited our selection. Finally I saw an ad where the price was reasonable, only $39.00, but still much higher than the 30 marks we had paid in Wuppertal. The exchange rate at that time was a little more than four to one, that is 4.25 German marks equaled 1 Canadian dollar. The price in German marks for this apartment would have been 165.75 marks. It seemed like an enormous amount of money at the time, because we still considered the value of money in German marks. The ad mentioned that the place was furnished; as we had no furniture then, this was the ideal solution to our problem. Knowing nothing about the city, we had no idea where that house was located. That this was one of the poorest districts we discovered later, but it wouldn't have mattered much where we lived, as we couldn't afford anything better.

"Please tell me how to get to that address?" I asked the desk clerk.

"There is a number 5 bus going down 97th street. You can catch it on Jasper Avenue going east. Then get off at 108th Street. It's not difficult to find," the clerk explained.

It was most important to save every penny we possibly could, as we only had $200.00 left from the sale of our lease after having paid a part of the passage. We had exchanged German marks for Canadian dollars to help us get over the rough spots in the beginning, having to buy so many things anew. I left Kurt and Andre at the hotel and set out to find the place. It was not complicated, as streets and avenues were in sequence with streets going north-south and avenues east-west.

33

The address was an ordinary looking two-story house. A huge, impressive basilica stood not far away at the opposite street corner. I saw a grocery store a few houses away. That would be convenient. The landlord led me to the basement. There were several doors. He opened one of them. The man explained that other families also lived in that basement. It certainly was a tiny place and, although there were two rooms, together they were not larger than one. A queen sized bed stood in one room, and the other was a kitchen with a stove, built-in cupboards, a sink, table and two chairs, and barely enough room to turn around. Both rooms had a tiny window. The toilet was at the opposite side of the basement and had to be shared with the other basement tenants. The door to our apartment didn't have a key to lock from the outside, only a latch inside. It certainly was not what I had expected, but it would have to do until Kurt was working again so we could afford something better. The landlord wanted the rent money for one month, so I paid him.

"I found the place and paid for it," I told Kurt upon my return to the hotel. "It's a dreadful place, but we'll have to make do until you have a job and the first pay. It seems that rents are much higher here than in Germany. The landlord said that we can move in immediately."

We checked out of the hotel. Moving into our new abode was simple enough, as we only had our hand luggage, so there was not much to unpack.

34

In the evening we were in for a surprise. Hearing a noise outside our door, I opened and discovered that a few young men were camped in front of our door. They had sleeping bags spread out over mattresses on the floor. When they saw me, they waved and smiled. Frightened by the unexpected discovery, I immediately closed the door again.

"Kurt, some young men are camped outside our door," I related. "What are we going to do? Do you think they will harm us?"

"Don't be silly. We'll just lock our door from the inside," Kurt replied casually. "That landlord sure knows how to squeeze money from tenants. He seems to rent out every little nook and cranny," he added with a grin.

The men were gone next morning, but returned each night. We also met some of the other basement occupants. A very tall Indian caught Andre's attention. Our son, with his hands in the pockets of his short pants, stalked around the strange man, looking him up and down and inspecting every inch. He was puzzled as he had never seen a man with braids. The young fellow in turn thought it rather funny to be the object of so much attention. He started to laugh.

"Good morning, young man," he said in a friendly tone of voice, smiling. "What's your name?" Of course Andre did not understand a word of what was said to him.

"That is Andre," I introduced my son. "He doesn't speak any English yet. We just arrived from Germany."

Kurt went out to look for a job in the morning. The gentleman at the immigration office had given him an address, which was within walking distance, where he should apply. It was a company where a great number of German immigrants were employed; language would not be a problem there. Kurt was hired and had to start the next morning.

In the meantime, I began cleaning the place, washing the windows and the cupboards inside and out. Suddenly, someone was frantically knocking on our door. Who could that be? A little scared, I opened a slit and discovered an old woman standing outside. She was gesticulating, talking continuously and finally pulling my arm. I did not understand a single word of what she was saying. At that point I had no idea what language she spoke, but it certainly wasn't English, German or French. Obviously she wanted something from me, since she was dragging me along upstairs. I heard a telephone ring and ring. She pointed to the receiver. Finally I grasped the reason she so desperately wanted me to come. I was supposed to answer the telephone. That day was my third in this city and I certainly didn't feel qualified to answer a telephone. It was difficult enough to follow a conversation or ask a question. Reluctantly I lifted the receiver and said "hello".

Luckily I understood most of what the caller said. When the landlady returned, I relayed the message. She thanked me for taking the call.

"My mother doesn't speak any English," she explained. "She only speaks Ukrainian."

Now I knew what language the lady spoke. "Did your mother just arrive from the old country?" I inquired, wondering why the old woman had been left alone.

"Oh, no, she has lived here for about fifty years, but refuses to learn English," the lady replied smiling.

The rest of our luggage was delivered the next day. It was a wooden crate. Nothing was missing. What a relief! Finally we had our own bed linens and towels and other things we needed.

At the corner grocery store I tried again to buy rye bread, but had no luck. After gathering the most necessary groceries for cooking our first meal I asked the store owner. "Where can I find a store that sells household items?"

We had left our blankets, dishes and many other implements in the apartment in Wuppertal. They were sold together with all our furniture. Now we urgently needed blankets and pillows and the most necessary items to run a household efficiently.

"The *Army and Navy* would be the store for you. They sell everything. Go south on 97th street or take the bus. You can't miss it. It's on your left," she explained.

"Kurt, let's go to buy a few things we need," I called out upon his return from work. There was still an hour left before closing time. Last night we had used what we had in our suitcases for sleeping.

We all walked about five blocks until we discovered a huge building with the name '*Army and Navy Department Store*' painted on the outside. It looked a bit run-down, but the store seemed to have all kinds of merchandize from clothing to household items. Everything was inexpensive. A sign said '*we undersell everybody*'. I picked up whatever we most urgently needed, and walked to the cashier. While waiting I read a sign on one of the pillars. It said: 'Sales clerks needed, apply within'.

"Kurt, they are looking for sales persons. I'm going to see if I can get a job here."

"But you have no experience and what about Andre?" he looked aghast as if I had lost my mind.

"It won't hurt to ask," I snapped back. "I could work part time."

"All right, ask. They won't take you. I can guarantee you that."

My English must have been sufficient, because I was hired to work on a two-week trial basis on Thursday evenings and all day Saturday. Kurt would have to take care of Andre during that time.

"How did you manage that?" my husband inquired still awed about my brazenness. "Didn't they ask if you had any experience?"

"Sure, they did, but I told them that I had sometimes worked in my father's shop, which is not a complete lie."

Leaving the place I noticed a store across the street with a bakery sign. "Kurt, there is a bakery. Let's see if they sell rye bread."

It was most fortunate for us that Mr. Adrian, a German baker, had recently started a business selling rye bread and a variety of cakes. The sales personnel spoke German. That store with all those mouth-watering cakes on display presented a great temptation. We bought some to take with us. I never went home from work afterwards without buying some of these goodies much to the detriment of my waistline.

Kurt had become acquainted with a fellow cabinet-maker during the two weeks he worked for that lumber company. One day the young man, whose brother was employed at the German consulate, told him that a gentleman had inquired about German cabinet-makers. This fellow was looking for people to do finishing work on his new house. The young man had asked Kurt, if he would be interested in a partnership doing that job.

"Do you think I should do it?" Kurt asked after telling me about the offer. "I would like to get out of the place where I'm working right now, because the pay is lousy, but it would mean taking a risk. When the job is done what will I do then? Perhaps I won't find other employment. I doubt that this company I'm working for now would take me back. You don't earn enough to pay the bills with the few hours of work every week, and I won't qualify for unemployment insurance. They tell me at work that it is difficult to find employment, especially during the winter."

"It's a tricky question, but I think you should give it a try. We have taken so many risks and everything turned out all right, why not?" Now I had stuck my neck out again. What if this job didn't turn out? The money I was making at the *Army and Navy* was not nearly enough to get by. If I could work full time then perhaps we could manage in case of emergency, but someone had to look after Andre.

8. SURPRISES

Kurt went to see the gentleman, who was looking for cabinetmakers. This gentleman, being a Jew, spoke German. He was looking for German craftsmanship. They came to an agreement.

The following week Kurt quit his job to start his new assignment together with the other fellow. He had to take the bus each day, and then walk down the street a fair distance, because the unfinished house was located on 149th Street.

40

We had been living in that tiny apartment for three weeks already. On that particular day I sat at the table in the kitchen reading something, Andre was asleep and Kurt at work. Everything was quiet, as most people were at work. Suddenly I heard a slight noise. Looking up I noticed that the door knob was slowly being turned from the outside. Terrified I jumped up from the chair. Was someone breaking in? I was alone with Andre. There was no other way out. Fear shot through me like lightening. There hadn't been a knock. I would have heard it. Then the door opened very quietly and the landlord stood in the doorway. Upon seeing me standing there his face turned red. His demeanour showed a guilty conscience. He stammered an apology, but it was so lame that no one would have believed him.

"I, I, I just wanted to check on the windows," he stuttered meekly. Then, taking a quick glance at the closed kitchen window, he left in a hurry. I sank back onto the kitchen chair, devastated. The shock was too much. What was the man looking for? We didn't own any great treasures. What did he have in mind? Had he only wanted to snoop around? If he had knocked, the situation would have been different, but his behaviour left no doubt in my mind that his intentions were not honourable.

When Kurt returned from work I told him about the incident.

"We'll have to find some other place, even if it costs a little more. I don't feel safe here. We can't even

41

lock the door when we go away." I said. "This place is terrible."

"There must be something better than this hole," Kurt agreed.

And so we started again searching for better accommodation. A few blocks away we found a four-story apartment house, which had a 'for rent' sign on it. That place seemed to be a better arrangement, than the one we had at the present, but it was more expensive - $45.00 a month. It consisted of two rooms, which were of normal size and was also furnished. The bathroom had to be shared with another couple on the same floor. There was a bathtub in it, a luxury I had sorely missed for a long time. We decided to take it and move in immediately, despite the fact that I had paid rent for four weeks at the present place. We could have stayed there another week, but were anxious to move out as soon as possible. Transporting our few belongings posed no problem. The brother of Kurt's partner, who worked at the German consulate, came with his V.W. to help us transport the wooden crate to the new place. The rest we carried.

Things were looking up. Kurt was working and I had my job on Thursdays and Saturdays. At a second-hand store we purchased a used couch for next to nothing. It was not completely clean anymore, but at the *Army and Navy* I found some slip covers with a large flower pattern to drape over. This made it look like new. It was our first item of furniture. Andre needed a place to sleep, so this couch was used during the day for sitting and became a bed at night.

"There is a letter from Wilfried," I called out, as I entered the apartment coming home from work one evening. "According to the address he is in Montreal. Let's see what he writes."

Wilfried had decided to try his luck in Montreal, Quebec. After receiving our letter with the new address, which my parents had forwarded to him, he wrote to us. I opened the envelope and began to read aloud:

"Dear Helga, Kurt and Andre,

Hope you are all in good health. I arrived in Montreal three weeks ago. So far I have been unable to find work here. How is the situation in Edmonton? Is there any possibility of finding employment?

Please answer quickly because I am running out of money soon and may be forced to return to Germany.

All the best,

Wilfried.

"We can use another hand. He could work with us. There is enough to do to keep us busy until spring. Write to him and tell him to come," Kurt suggested.

That same evening I wrote a letter to my brother telling him to come as soon as possible. I mailed it the next morning. We figured that he should be here within a few days. I suddenly realized how much I missed him and could hardly wait for his arrival. We had been so busy with all the new developments that I had not given it much thought. It would feel so good to have a member of my family living close.

9. LEARNING THE ROPES

The new apartment was a more suitable home than the one we had before. The place looked comfortable and cosy with the purchase of the second-hand couch. We also became acquainted and developed a good relationship with our neighbours, Art and Faye. They were a friendly couple with two boys, David and Wayne, who were a little older than our son.

One Saturday, Art, who was an outdoors enthusiast, came over to ask if we would like to come along to the lake on Sunday. Of course we were delighted about the prospect to see the countryside. Having no car of our own, it was an opportunity we didn't want to miss. We were also eager to learn as much as possible about the surrounding area.

During peace times in Germany such an outing usually involved a visit to a nice restaurant after a leisurely walk around the lake. There we would order a cup of coffee and choose from one of those mouth-watering pieces of cake or torte the restaurant had to offer. It was always an occasion to wear nice clothing. We therefore dressed accordingly, putting on our best outfits and polished shoes.

"Are you ready to go?" Art called out in the hallway.

"Yes, we are," we replied in unison.

When he saw us he gasped, and looked at us disapprovingly. "You should have put on some old clothing," he scolded, "it's rough out there, but let's go, otherwise it will get too late. You just have to be extra careful not to rip your nylons."

We thoroughly enjoyed the car ride. It was the end of September. The summer heat had given way to a tepid breeze. A strong smell of moist, rotting leaves hung in the air. The foliage was exploding in all nuances from red to yellow. High up in the air was a flock of geese gathering for the long flight south. Everywhere on the vast fields were farmers busy with the harvest.

Art explained that we were driving to Miquelon Lake. He had a little row boat there. Upon arrival we noticed the surrounding area of the lake. It was wild and rugged. There was no sign of any paved or groomed walkways or fancy restaurant. Art took out his fishing gear. Then we all walked to the lake shore following a dirt path, and stepped into the little row boat, except Faye. She decided that fishing was 'not her cup of tea', as she put it, and that she would rather stay at the shore to read a book.

The boat ride was leisurely. Art was paddling far out to the middle of the lake. Then he stopped and opened a little metal box. It had a number of fish hooks inside. He took his fishing rod, and fastened one of the hooks.

"Here take this one," he said, handing me the rod he had baited.

"But I've never done any fishing. I don't know how," I protested. He laughed and showed me how to throw the line. I held on to the rod. Before long there was a pull. Beginners luck, of course.

"Now reel in the line," Art called out. I did what I was told and sure enough I had caught a fish. Art took it off the hook and fastened the live fish on a line in the water.

"Don't you kill it first? It will hurt when it is hanging on the line," I cried out in agony, realizing that the fish was hooked on the line and could not get away. How brutal, I thought, but Art just laughed. "That fish doesn't feel a thing," he said casually.

I was not so sure about it. The realization that the fish was not killed immediately to end its suffering took the fun out of fishing for me. I handed the rod to Kurt. "Here, take it," I said. "I don't want to fish anymore."

Afterwards we sat at the shore for a while enjoying the sun before driving back to the city. Art gave us some fish to cook at home. I never understood the fascination for fishing, but will not forget Art's kindness taking these poor immigrants to the lake. It was a heartwarming experience. Kurt liked fishing. He later built a little row boat and went several times out to a lake. We both realized that old garments would have been more suitable for the occasion. Next time we would know better.

10. MISSED OPPORTUNITY

One evening we were studying the newspaper ads looking for a good deal on used furniture. By chance my eyes glanced at an ad that advertised a 3 acre lot for sale at the asking price of $500.00.

"Kurt, we should take a look at that place. It has a little house on it. Perhaps we can buy it."

"But we only have a little over $300.00 in our account at the bank. The ad says that the seller wants $500.00," Kurt replied.

"He might take the $300.00 as a down payment and we can pay the rest in installments instead of paying rent each month. We could also try to get a loan from the bank."

"It would clean us out completely. We would have no nest egg left. And you know that I don't want to go into debt," Kurt cautioned. "Furthermore I doubt that the bank would lend us any money. We don't have a credit rating and no collateral."

"It wouldn't hurt to see the place. There is a telephone number. I will phone and ask for the address."

That evening I went down to the landlady and asked to use the phone. The gentleman, who answered my call, told me that we could see the place whenever we wanted to. It was empty and not locked. He told me to ask the people, who lived in the trailer on the same property, for details, and to show us the place.

The address was at the outskirt of the city in the Beverly district.

It was a Sunday morning in October when we took the bus to Beverly. The property was in walking distance from the bus stop and easy to find. Most of the large area was covered with grass and some bushes. It looked wild and uncared for. We noticed the trailer on the property. Some people sat outside on lawn chairs. They seemed to enjoy the tepid autumn sun with a bottle of beer and conversation. A few children were playing ball. At the other end of the property we could see a little house. It reminded me of a chicken coop, because it was very small.

"That must be the place," I remarked. "Let's talk to these people."

After we introduced ourselves they were very friendly, treating us like we were old friends and offering a bottle of beer. It was too early in the day to drink and we declined.

"The owner told us that we could look at the house. Is it alright to go inside?" I asked.

"Go right ahead. Look around as much as you like. It's not locked because nobody has lived there for a long time. It may be a little dirty right now. If you have any questions, we'll be glad to answer them. We would love to have you move in. My wife likes company and would gladly take care of the little fellow while you are working," the man offered without asking his better half.

48

These people seemed anxious to have company. They were talkative and I had a problem following their torrent of words. The area was still at the outskirts of the city and sparsely populated.

Then we walked over to the place. The outside was covered with wooden boards, which originally were painted white, but had discoloured to a dirty grey. The roof seemed to be strong enough to last for another year or two. Kurt examined it thoroughly. In front of the entrance was a screen door. It hung a little crooked on the hinges. The screen was ripped at one place. Kurt could easily fix it, if we decided to buy the property. Shrubs had grown wild around the little house. There was no basement. It was obvious that the place had not been occupied for a very long time. Upon stepping inside we noticed utter chaos. The people had not exaggerated when they mentioned that it was 'a little dirty'. It was not only a little, but very dirty. The kitchen cupboards had numerous tiny brown spots all over from the excrement of flies. A few old cups and plates were still inside. Spider webs hung from the ceiling. Old torn curtains were haphazardly fastened on the windows, which were too dirty to see much of the outside. The linoleum floor urgently needed washing, as a lot of soil was caked on. There was a nauseating smell from having stood empty over a long period of time. The house had a tiny kitchen and two normal sized rooms. Electricity was installed, but not turned on. The toilet consisted of a ramshackle outhouse. We discovered a large metal container attached to the house while walking around the outside; its purpose escaped our imagination.

49

"I wonder what that is for," Kurt said examining the contraption. "We have to ask the people. They would know."

"I think a good scrubbing would make it possible to live here. Next year we could build a proper house on it," I contemplated.

"You don't even know if we can get it. How are we going to manage the rest of the expenses? We could lose our shirts." Kurt replied stroking his chin. It would be a gamble. He had enough work to last until spring, but what would happen afterwards was anyone's guess. I didn't know if the *Army and Navy* would keep me over the winter months, because my colleagues had told me that many sales clerks were laid off after Christmas.

"Let's talk to the people again," I said and started walking back to the trailer.

"Do you know what that large metal container is used for?" I asked the lady.

"That is the water tank. We don't have water here. The waterman brings water when we phone him," she explained.

I had never heard of water being delivered by truck. Usually there was a pump or a well, when waterlines were not installed yet. I simply could not fathom how that would work. Would the water be clean enough to drink? What if one ran out and was unable to get a filling in time of need? How much would it cost to have it brought in? Doubts began to

50

manifest. This deal didn't seem quite so tempting anymore. We would have to think about it a little longer. There were too many problems that needed solving. Perhaps it would be better to wait for another opportunity.

On our way home we passed a house with a sign indicating a Chinese restaurant. "I'm getting hungry. Let's get something to eat," Kurt suggested.

We stepped inside. It was a tiny room with only two tables. An older Chinese gentleman greeted us. He seemed to be the only person running the place. There was no cook or waitress as far as we could make out and no other patrons.

"You want Chinese specialty?" he asked in a friendly tone of voice. "I make you something veeery good."

"Yes, please bring us something to eat. We are hungry," Kurt replied.

The gentleman disappeared to the next room, which was most likely the kitchen. We could hear him working there with pots and pans. After a while he returned carrying three plates of steaming hot rice with a mixture of vegetables and meat on top. We tried to use the wooden sticks he had put beside the forks and spoons. I must admit that I have never tasted anything so delicious. It was the best Chinese food I ever ate. The Chinese gentleman, smiling all over his face, enjoyed seeing our appetite. He bowed several times while we ate.

"You like Chinese food?" he asked.

"Oh, yes, that is very tasty," I praised his cooking skills.

"You come back?"

"We'll try," I promised.

On the way home we decided not to advance our negotiations for buying the property. Perhaps it would have worked out, but it could have also brought us to the brink of destitution. We might have encountered severe hardship when unexpected expenses occurred. One thing is sure we would have been desperately short of money for a long time. In the end it was too much of a gamble and we let it go. It might have made us very rich, but we could have also lost what little we had. We'll never know. I often wondered how our lives had turned out if we had taken the risk and bought the property. It was only a few years later that the entire area was developed, and apartment buildings constructed. Whoever was fortunate enough to have the money to buy the property outright may have become a millionaire.

11. THE STRANGER

Approximately two weeks had passed since I wrote to Wilfried. We were already wondering if he had received my letter. It shouldn't take him that long to get here. We had counted three days for the train and two days for the letter to arrive. The postal service was usually very prompt. Why was there such delay?

Then one evening, when we had just sat down to eat supper, someone knocked on the door. There stood Wilfried together with another man, who was older than my brother, perhaps in his thirties. I had an instant dislike for the fellow, although I could not explain why. He was polite enough and behaved like any other person. The men looked tired and exhausted, their hair was dishevelled and clothes besmeared with dirt. They probably hadn't shaved for several days. Wilfried introduced the man and told us that they had been on the same ship, the *Arosa Sun*, and sat at the same table at dinner. After going ashore they had met, and decided to rent a room together, as it was cheaper for two people than for one.

After a big hello and embrace, we all sat down at the table.

"We want to wash up a bit," Wilfried said getting up again.

I showed him where everything was, and handed him a towel. After both men had cleaned up, I took out two additional plates and cutlery, placing them in front of the new arrivals.

"Let's eat now. Tell us all about your trip. If we had known when you were coming, we could have picked you up at the station."

"We didn't come by train. We hitchhiked because we were running out of money. I'm sure glad that you have work and a home already. We'll quickly have to find a place to stay. You obviously don't have any room for us here."

"I'll ask our landlord. Perhaps he has another room for rent," I offered.

"That would be perfect," Wilfried replied glad to get help.

After supper I went downstairs with him to talk to the landlord. He did indeed have an empty room available in the basement. Wilfried rented it with the last dollars he had and the two men moved in.

Next morning Wilfried accompanied Kurt to work on the unfinished house, and the stranger went out to look for a job. Over the next few weeks I had to feed two more adults until Wilfried received his first pay check. My brother was able to contribute to the expenses, but the stranger could not. He simply had no money. Food was not very expensive, but, with the little we had, cooking for two more men made a difference. One evening we were talking about it at dinnertime. Wilfried suggested they take Andre along so I could work full time. There was already heat in the house in case it got cold. Andre would have plenty of room to play. They would give him hammer and nails and pieces of wood so he had something to do. This solution suited me well. Management at the *Army and Navy* was happy to employ me full time, as the high school girls, who worked there during the summer, were back in school.

54

The man, who had accompanied Wilfried, did not find any work. He went out every day, but when I asked him upon his return if he had found something, he always shook his head. "No, I havn't. Tomorrow I will try again," was his steady answer.

Several weeks had passed already, but the stranger still hadn't found any work. I was getting impatient. Everybody was working except this man. He didn't talk much, and when asked questions skillfully avoided a direct answer. How long could we carry him? He was not related to us. As a matter of fact, we knew very little about him. It certainly was not our problem. I began to resent his presence.

The immigration office was only a few blocks away from the *Army and Navy*. I decided to go there and ask for help. During my lunch hour I went to see the friendly young man, who had greeted us at the train station. Unfortunately there was a different official in the office that day, who didn't speak any German. I had to explain everything in English, which was still a little difficult.

"What can I do for you?" he asked in a friendly tone of voice.

"My brother Wilfried arrived from Montreal. He was accompanied by a man, who had been on the same ship. They both have rented a room in the building where we live. Wilfried has work, but the other fellow can't find a job. I have been cooking for the man, but we have little money, and can't afford to feed a stranger. The Government of Canada should be

55

looking after him. After all they brought him over. Can't you do something for the fellow?"

"Of course we will help him. Tell him to come and see us, but he must bring his papers and passport," the official advised.

I thanked the gentleman and left. In the evening I gave the stranger the message.

"I went to the immigration office today, and was told that you would get help from them. You must go there with your passport and papers. They will find a job for you or give you coupons for food."

"Yes, I'll go there tomorrow," the man promised.

At supper time the next day he did not show up. We waited a while, but then sat down to eat. The man did not appear at all that evening and Kurt casually remarked," perhaps, they found him a job somewhere out of town."

In the morning Wilfried came for breakfast and told us that the man had disappeared. Without leaving a message he had taken his suitcase and all his belongings. He must have left the place after Wilfried had gone to work. We were all glad to be rid of him. Wilfried had the room for himself now, and I didn't need to cook for the man.

"After all you have done for him he could have at least said goodbye or written a 'thank you' note,"

Wilfried mumbled, but he too was glad to be rid of the fellow. I didn't give the matter another thought.

A few days passed. I was at work when the same official, I had visited at the immigration office, came to see me.

"Are you Mrs. Tucque?" he asked.

"Yes I am. What is it all about?" I replied surprised about the fact that this man would come to see me at work. What could he possibly want from me?

"Do you have a brother by the name of Wilfried Maul?"

"Yes. Has anything happened to him?" I asked alarmed that Wilfried might have had an accident.

"No, he is not hurt. The R.C.M.P. has picked him up in the vicinity of Winnipeg."

"But that is impossible! Wilfried is here in Edmonton. We had breakfast together only a few hours ago. How can he be in Winnipeg?" I replied aghast.

"That is really strange. We'll have to look into the matter further. Something isn't right here," the gentleman replied looking startled. "Where is your brother now?"

"He is at work with my husband. They will both be home at suppertime," I explained.

"Does your brother live with you?"

"Yes, he lives in the same house and eats with us," I explained.

"I like to have a word with him and your husband. May I visit you this evening?"

"Yes, of course. Come at about 7 o'clock. I'm sure they will all be at home then."

The official showed up at the designated hour. He asked for Wilfried's passport and papers. After examining them very carefully he commented: "Everything seems to be in order here, but we have to be sure that you are the person in this passport. The picture looks like you, but the passport could have been stolen and altered. We have to be absolutely certain that you are that person. Do you have any photos with the family together?"

We searched our few belongings for photos and discovered one with the entire family.

"May I have this for a few days? I promise to return it," he begged.

"I still don't understand what the problem is," I remarked, as I felt that there was no reason for the mistrust. The papers were all in order.

"The man, who was picked up by the R.C.M.P., was hitchhiking. As a matter of fact the squad car had noticed him standing at the road, and given him a ride.

When asked by the officers to show them his passport or identification, he said that his passport had been stolen and that his name was Wilfried Maul. They are keeping him in jail until the matter is cleared up."

Everything became crystal clear now. *What a nerve, I thought, after all the help we had given the stranger, to lie to the police and pretend to be Wilfried.* My premonition had been correct. I had a dislike for the man from the moment he stepped into our home. He was an impostor.

"But that is the fellow I came to see you about a few days ago," I blurted out. "Don't you remember?"

"We have so many visitors every day. Now that you mention it I do seem to remember. I had no idea that this is the fellow you were talking about. You came to ask us to help the man find a job. Yes, I remember it now."

"That is the man," I agreed.

"Now I understand. Don't worry, everything seems to be in order here, but we have to follow regulations to be sure that what you said is true. I will return the photo in a few days. I'm certain that the matter will all be straightened out soon."

The official returned after about a week. We all sat together at the table.

"We have checked all the details and everything is in order at your end. R.C.M.P. officials have contacted German authorities. The culprit is still in jail, and will be extradited shortly. He had been denied entry into Canada, because he was incarcerated in Germany for theft a few years back. Apparently he has a wife and two children back home. He must have come as a stowaway. There were no records of him on the ship, where he said he was a passenger. How that was possible is not as yet clear. The authorities are still checking the case. Perhaps he had help from someone outside."

"It would have never occurred to me that he wasn't a regular passenger, because he ate at our table in the dining room, but I never saw his cabin. But I remember the first day. There was a commotion at dinner with the seating arrangement, one plate was missing. After he raised his voice, the waiter brought another plate and apologized. We were not closely acquainted on the boat, but he stood there and spoke to me when I came on land," Wilfried related.

My brother is a sociable and helpful individual, who never dreams that someone would take advantage of his good nature. This incident taught him a lesson.

The matter was finally concluded, but it had been the cause for some concern and sleepless nights. We never heard from the stranger again.

12. ANDRE

It was late in the afternoon. I was working at the store, helping a customer find the items she was looking for, when Kurt and Wilfried appeared. They looked rather distraught. I immediately sensed that something was wrong.

"Where is Andre?" I asked sharply.

"We thought he might be with you," they sheepishly replied.

"How can he be here? You took him to work," I shouted angrily.

"We lost him."

"How could you lose him?" I yelled frantically. "Don't you care? You were supposed to look after him. What's the matter with you guys?"

"We were walking along 149th Street. Andre was running ahead of us like he always does. We called and ordered him to wait, but he wouldn't listen. Then the bus arrived. We were still too far away to reach it in time, but we could see Andre getting on. Then the bus took off without waiting for us. We waved to the driver, but he probably didn't see us, or was in a hurry," Kurt explained.

I was almost out of my mind with fear. My hands were shaking. What if someone took our son and did him harm? Andre was still so little. All he could say was his name. So far he had only learned a few words in English, not enough to make himself understood. Even if people had good intentions, it would be difficult for them to know where he belonged. All probable scenarios raced through my mind. The little five years old lost in a strange city unable to speak the language. The thought was unbearable.

61

"I'll have to call the police. They have to start looking for him right now." I cried out in desperation, tears were rolling down my cheeks. My heart was beating so fast that I could hardly breathe. The fear almost choked me.

Kurt and Wilfried were still discussing our options when a lady from the office approached.

"Helga, your landlady just called to say that your son is with her. She wanted to know if you will be coming home soon."

"Thank God he is safe," I cried out relieved. "I must get home quickly. He will be frightened being alone with the landlady." It was close to quitting time, so there was no problem taking the time off. I grabbed my sweater and purse. A bus just happened to come when we stepped out of the store. It was only a short distance ride and then we ran the rest of the way.

Andre was all right. He was sitting with the landlady in her living room. She had given him some picture books to look at, and was talking to him in a friendly way. He didn't seem to be upset. After embracing him I asked: "How did you find your way home?"

"I stepped into the bus, because Papa and Wilfried didn't come. I didn't want to wait any longer. At the transfer point I stepped out where we always do. The next bus came right away, so I stepped in and the bus drove off."

"Why didn't you wait for Papa and Wilfried?"

"I wanted to see you, but you were not at home."

"How did you know that it was the correct bus and where to get out?" I questioned him.

"It had the number 5 on it," he answered proudly having learned numbers already.

"Didn't the bus driver ask you where your parents were? How could you get on without anyone being with you?"

"I just sat down. Nobody talked to me."

"Weren't you afraid?"

"No, only when I couldn't find you here."

The arrangement of Kurt taking Andre to work obviously was not working too well. Luckily I soon found a German lady, who was willing to look after the little guy during the day. Most of the money I earned was now paid for babysitting.

13. RUDE AWAKENING

There were no windows in the basement of the *Army and Navy* department store. Therefore I was in for a great surprise when, on a day in late October, I stepped out of the store at 6 p.m. A drastic drop in temperature had taken place during that day. It had been warm enough in the morning, so I didn't take a coat to work. Now an icy wind swept through the streets, hurling dust and dry leaves in the crisp autumn air. People wrapped scarves around their faces to escape the wind's fury. I couldn't believe the change that had come over the city since the morning hours. Shivering with cold I waited for the bus. Walking was impossible without warm clothing. When I arrived at the street corner, I ran the short distance home. The landlord was balancing on a high ladder in front of the building, installing storm windows. He waved to me as I entered the building.

"Look out of the window," Kurt called out upon waking up the next morning. "It's white outside."

A foot of snow had fallen over night. The thermometer showed twenty degrees below zero Fahrenheit. It was an eye opener for us. We had never experienced such sudden drop in temperature before, not even at home at the foot of the Giant Mountains of Silesia, where some winters were severe. The cold weather had never come so quickly and unexpectedly.

This was only October. We stood at the window admiring the beauty of sparkling snow crystals, as the sun was now shining brightly from a clear blue sky.

"It looks lovely, like a fairy tale world of ice and snow," I exclaimed excitedly. "But we'll have to buy warm clothing quickly. Our coats are not warm enough for such temperatures. It will cost us a bundle."

Kurt, Andre and Helga at Christmas 1957

14. MOVING AGAIN

Winter didn't seem to come to an end. We were all getting tired of walking through slush and mud on the streets. But then one day a warm wind was blowing. The crispness in the air had disappeared. It felt like spring. Everywhere melting water was running down the streets. Slowly the temperature began to rise.

Kurt and Wilfried had finished their work on the house. There were no new assignments. They went out every day looking for a job, but nothing was available. I studied the ads in the newspaper day after day, but there was nothing listed until one day I discovered an ad by *Simpson Sears Department stores*. They were looking for a furniture refinisher.

"Isn't that something you could do?" I asked Kurt.

"I could do it, but remember that I'm colour-blind. What will happen if I don't come up with the right shade and put green instead of a red shade on or vice versa?"

"You don't have to tell them that you are colour-blind. Give it a try. If it doesn't work out, they may have something else for you to do."

Wilfried, Andre and Kurt

Kurt went for an interview. He had already learned enough English to make himself understood. His qualifications as a German cabinet maker put him on top of the list. He was hired for repairs of minor dents and scratches on furniture damaged during transport. We were safe again and decided to look for a better apartment, one without furniture. We had already bought some items and were now ready to buy box bases and mattresses for all of us. We discovered a basement suite with a bathroom for us alone. It seemed ideal. The rent was $50.00 per month, which was very reasonable for that type of apartment. With both of us working it was affordable.

This time we needed a larger vehicle for the move, but a friend helped out. The box bases and mattresses were bought and delivered to the new place.

The apartment looked very nice after moving in and setting up the furniture. I was happy to finally have a respectable place again. Tired from the move we went to bed early. We must have been asleep for about three hours when a noise above our bedroom woke us.

"It sounds as if someone is rocking in a chair. I hope that doesn't go on all night. I can't sleep with the constant noise," I said to Kurt.

"This person has to go to bed soon. It's after midnight already. Let's try to ignore it."

We tried to get back to sleep again, but it was impossible. The rocking went on all night. Next day we felt as if we hadn't slept at all. Going to work was a challenge. In the evening after returning from work I asked the landlady what that noise was about.

"My daughter is mentally challenged. She does not sleep at night. She sits in the rocking chair and rocks," she replied, giving me a strange look.

That explained why the rent was reasonable. The landlord must have had a problem keeping renters. A person had to be completely deaf to sleep with the racket going on all night. We tried to ignore the rocking, but it did not work. Soon we became grumpy and nervous wrecks.

"I can't go on much longer," Kurt said one day. "I need to get my sleep. We have to find a house to rent where we are alone."

And so we started searching the ads again. There was an old farm house for rent at the outskirts of the city. The price was a lot more than we had in mind to pay, $75.00 per month, but then decided that it would be worth getting a good night's sleep to retain our sanity. There would be no one above us anymore.

The new landlord was of German descent and could speak the language. The house was empty already and we were allowed to move in at the first of the month.

Kurt borrowed a truck to move our furniture. The house had a living room, kitchen and two bedrooms. There was also a toilet inside. From the living room one could walk through a long hall all the way to the kitchen, which was located at the other end. Outside was a large yard with a vegetable garden patch and a shed. Some Saskatoon bushes grew near the window. One day in July a neighbour lady came to see me, asking if she would be allowed to pick Saskatoons. At first I didn't understand what she was talking about never having heard that name before, but she pointed to the bush in front.

"Of course, you can pick all you want. What do you want to do with them? Can one eat them?" I asked surprised.

"You can make pies with them," she explained. "Have you never eaten a Saskatoon pie?"

"No, I've never even heard of it. I don't think they grow in Germany."

It was not long after that conversation when the lady brought me a pie to try. It tasted delicious. I baked Saskatoon pies every year from there on.

Helga in front of the farm house

Since Andre was able to walk he had been told that, as soon as we were living in a house, he would be allowed to make as much noise as he wanted to. Nobody would scold him, if he ran around and jumped on the floor. In Germany we had always lived on the top floor. The people living underneath often complained of too much noise. In order to keep the peace we had tried to occupy our son with quiet entertainment, so he would not jump around too much. Usually I took him for long walks during the day to use up his abundance of energy. Now we had to stick to our promise. It was as if a wild animal was released from his cage. Andre ran from one end of the house to the other back and forth, jumping over the couch and other furniture, summersaulting and screaming on top of his lungs for several hours. It was nerve wrecking, but we did not say a word. He had to get all his pent-up frustration out of his system. Finally, his energy spent, he dropped on his bed and quickly fell asleep.

15. THE WILDCAT

We were returning from work that evening. Approaching the house in the dreary fading light, we noticed a grey bundle in the snow close to the main door. It was the end of March. Snow covered the ground. The evenings were still rather cold, dropping down to the minus degrees. Upon closer inspection, we discovered a huge cat. It looked dead. But when we approached there seemed to be a slight movement.

"Oh, the poor thing. It must be very ill. We should take it inside. It will freeze out here. I wonder where it came from."

"It's awfully big. I've never seen such a huge cat. Look at the paws. They're like the ones of a large dog," Kurt commented. Having come from Europe, we were surprised that housecats would grow to such a size. However, many creatures were so much bigger in Canada than in the old country – deer, elk and especially mosquitos – so it did not seem inconceivable that cats were too.

Kurt picked up the almost lifeless body and carried it inside. He gently laid it down on the kitchen floor. Andre stroked its fur, but it growled a little, just a feeble attempt as if to say, "I don't want to be touched."

70

"Leave it alone," I told him. "The cat is too ill and probably does not want to be petted right now."

"We must get a sandbox, Kurt said, walking outside to the shed where some old crates were stored. One of them was large enough to fit the cat. He filled it with sand. "That should do it," he commented setting down the box near the entrance door. The cat lay there not moving at all.

"That must be an old tomcat. I can't remember ever seeing such a huge one," I said. "I wonder to whom it belongs."

"Maybe it's been living in the wild. Someone may have thrown it out or it had run away, who knows? It most likely fended for itself," my husband replied sitting down on the couch to read the paper. "Just leave it be. It'll come around. It may have eaten something that didn't agree with it."

After a short while, the cat was sick again. Despite its deplorable condition, the creature managed to use the box this time. The cat lay there hardly moving at all. We placed an old blanket on the floor, a dish of water, and a few scraps of meat. The animal did not touch either.

The next morning showed some improvement in the cat's condition. It did not look quite as lifeless as the day before. Luckily it was a weekend so we were home. On the third day, the diarrhoea finally stopped. When we returned home from work that evening, we noticed that the cat had sipped a little water. It had also eaten from the food. That was a good sign. We began to hope for its recovery. Very soon the cat developed a ferocious appetite. Within a few days it was well again, walking regally through the rooms as if it were the owner. The animal's behaviour showed superiority, and it did not like to be petted.

For two weeks, the cat resided in our house never bothering any of us, but making it clear that it did not wish to be touched. It was Sunday afternoon. My husband was sitting on the front steps enjoying the warm sunshine after the long winter days. The cat lay beside him. This was its first time outside since it was found. A little dog leisurely strolled into the yard. Without provocation the cat leaped up. Within seconds it was sitting on the dog's back attacking the poor little pup. It happened so quickly that Kurt was taken by surprise. There was an earth-shaking scream. Kurt immediately jumped up grabbing the cat by the neck jerking it away from the frightened dog. It was in the nick of time. A few moments later the dog would have been dead. Kurt brought the cat indoors, and the wounded dog slowly dragged itself away from the property.

"We can't keep the cat, "I said. "This time it was a dog. What will happen when a little child comes to visit us? This cat could easily kill it."

"You're right. It's too dangerous. We'll take it to the forest. If it belongs somewhere it will find its way home, but it has probably lived on its own before, so it won't starve. It's also well fed now and healthy," Kurt replied.

We drove to the nearby forest. After we opened the car door, the cat gingerly stepped out, slowly making its way to the first trees. It turned around one more time, looking at us as if to say:" Thanks for saving my life." The big cat disappeared between the trees never to be seen again.

Years later I came across a photo of a bobcat. "Oh, for heaven's sake, I called out. "That looks like the cat we saved."

16. BONZO

For several months the skeletons of two 1946 Ford cars lay in our backyard. Radiators, tires, car seats, and other parts had been scattered all over the lawn and driveway or leaned against the shed of our rented old farmhouse. Kurt had often entered the house late in the evening, tired and exhausted and his coveralls, face and hands smeared with oil. Sometimes, when nothing seemed to work right, he had been in a bad mood and ready to throw in the towel. "Why am I doing that? I'm not a mechanic!" he had yelled. "I wish I'd never started it! How could I have been so stupid to think I would be able to build a car!"

Other times, when some progress was made, he'd come to the kitchen wiping the sweat from his forehead and commenting very proudly, "Finally I have solved the problem. Now I found out how these things fit together", or "That seems to be working all right." Then he found the courage to continue. The work progressed slowly, as disappointments and problems arose from inexperience and lack of expertise. Doubts crept up about whether or not this job was worth the effort, but after a lot of swearing and the occasional, "Yahoo, I have done it!" one fine-looking vehicle eventually emerged from the two carcasses.

The new car, or rather the old car, was black on the outside. It had shining chrome fenders as in 1946 cars were still built with genuine metal. On both sides were two doors and three windows, one elongated at the back and the windshield, of course. There was also a large trunk at the back. The seats were covered with light brown velour. It had a spacious interior. So it was possible to stretch our legs and sit comfortably. The vehicle was operated with a manual gearshift, four gears and one reverse gear, and the odometer still measured in miles.

It all began during the spring of 1959. Our neighbours, with whom we had become friends, had invited us for a cup of coffee one evening. The Johnsons resided in a converted railroad car, which they had transported to their lot. They were still busy renovating everything inside and out to transform it into a little house. A kitchen and two bedrooms were finished. Everything looked quite presentable. Irving Johnson was a handy person with artistic talent. With great skill he had painted an impressive mural on the kitchen wall, which gave the room a cozy look. The Johnsons were almost as poor as we were, but they possessed a vehicle. We envied them for having their own transportation. That evening we sat around the kitchen table while the kids were playing on the floor.

"Oh, I would love to drive to the mountains! I miss them so much," I sighed, homesick for the Giant Mountains of Silesia.

"For that you will have to wait a while because we won't be able to afford a car in the near future," Kurt answered.

"I might have a solution to your problem," Irving declared with a roguish grin. "Would you be interested?"

"Of course," Kurt replied.

"Mind you, it would involve a lot of work, but I'm certain you'll be able to do it. My brother had a car accident recently. The wreck is sitting in his yard. I'm sure the motor is still in good shape, but the body is a total write-off. You could buy another vehicle of the same year at the auto wreckers. I am certain they'll sell you one for only a few dollars. Then from the parts of the two you can build one that works.

"But I have no idea how to do that!"

"Kurt, you're a clever guy. Don't worry about it. It really isn't that difficult. I could probably lend you a hand."

"Irving, I am a cabinetmaker, not an auto mechanic!" Kurt retorted, horrified at the thought. "What will happen if I mess up?"

"Well? Then you'll have lost a few dollars. So what? That's not such a big deal. Just try it. I'm pretty sure you can do it. My brother doesn't want money for the vehicle because he would have to take it to the auto-wreckers. Giving it to you saves him the money for towing." It was understandable that Kurt did not feel confident, as he had never owned or repaired a car, but he decided to give it a try. He bought an old clunker at the auto wrecker. A tow truck towed the vehicle, as well as the damaged car from Irving's brother, to our back yard. And so, after a lot of sweat and upheaval, and Irving's occasional help, a means of transportation finally emerged. Washed and polished, the new-old car stood in wait for its maiden voyage. It was indeed an exciting day when a complete vehicle had finally emerged from the different parts. We christened it "Bonzo" and treated it almost like a member of the family. Sometimes we even talked to it, as if a car had a brain! Bonzo was our ticket to the mountains at a time when we were still dirt-poor.

Andre and Kurt with Bonzo

"Let's go for a ride! Bonzo is waiting," Kurt shouted. Andre ran to the car and climbed inside. I untied my apron and joined the fun. Everything went according to plan. No problems were encountered during the test drive. Kurt drove slowly around the neighbourhood, while we looked through the car's windows feeling like a king and queen enjoying the leisurely trip. Finally our dream had come true. We were the proud owners of a car!

"Bonzo will get us around town quite nicely. Maybe we can drive to the mountains soon," announced Kurt.

"When will we go to Jasper?" Andre asked impatiently.

"As soon as possible," his father replied. "But before we take off, I would like to build a little utility trailer from the remaining tires, so we can take some extra gas and tools along just in case we should have a mishap."

17. THE ADVENTURE ROAD

"Bonzo, be a good boy, and bring us back home safely," Kurt said, knocking the hood of our beloved addition. This was our first trip to the Rocky Mountains. We had borrowed a little tent and a camping stove, which we stowed away in the homemade trailer together with some gasoline containers, some spare parts and the toolbox. Food, dishes and clothing were placed in the trunk.

An ink-blue sky stretched as far as the eye could see when we started our drive. Indian paintbrush bloomed at the roadside in all shades of red. The sweet odour of clover and freshly cut grass hung in the air. Poplars grew in abundance everywhere, their thin, light green stems shimmering in the morning sun. A slight breeze fanned their leaves so they looked like a silver and green kaleidoscope. Here and there we saw a herd of cows leisurely grazing in the lush meadows. A hawk circled high up in the sky in search of its next meal. 'WATCHMAKER' was painted in big, white letters on the roof of a house near the road. Traffic was light during those years so long ago, and driving still a joy. Truck traffic was also much less than today, as highway #16 only led to Jasper, then highway #93 continued south through the National Park. Only a narrow dirt path existed at that time between Jasper and British Columbia, but it was dangerous and closed during the winter months. The only connection between Alberta and British Columbia was the Trans-Canada highway #1 over the Roger's Pass, in the south via the Crowsnest Pass or by railroad. Later the Yellowhead highway was built. Traffic has increased dramatically since. The numerous curves before Edson have also been straightened after a politician lost his life in one of those dangerous bends.

Shortly after passing the small town of Edson we could already make out the vague contours of the mountains in the distance. The scenery changed noticeably. Flatland turned into hilly landscape. The road climbed constantly.

A few miles after leaving the town of Hinton, we reached the park entrance. A little wooden house stood in the middle of the road with a sign announcing "Welcome to Jasper National Park". After paying the entrance fee of $2.00 for an entire year, we leisurely proceeded towards Jasper.

The colour of the mountains changed continuously. Sometimes they appeared grey then again in a somewhat lilac or bluish green tint. The road went along the blue Talbot Lake, its banks covered with white sand dunes. Then another lake came into view. It was olive green tinged, and smelled of sulfur. The triangular shaped top of Pyramid Mountain peeked through from behind a mountain chain. We were able to distinguish the fire watchtower on its summit.

Across from the entrance to the town of Jasper on the left side was the Cottonwood campground. It was the only campground in Jasper at that time. Tents were erected on a grass-covered area with camping tables scattered everywhere. A washhouse with toilets stood in the middle. We looked for a suitable table with enough space on the side to pitch our tent.

"Let's take a drive through Jasper," Kurt announced after setting up the tent.

Jasper was still a sleepy community. On the left side of the main road was the railroad station, where the transcontinental train passed through every day. A black, wooden statue of a bear with the name sign "Jasper", which is the symbol of the town, stood in front of it. Shops and the Astoria Hotel were located on the other side of the street. The Park Administration and pharmacy were also on that side. Life in Jasper was very relaxed. One was able to cross the street without any danger.

"I want to use a different route for our return drive," Kurt declared in the evening sitting at the camping table, and studying the map with the shine of the camp light, "but the road via Banff and highway #2 seems rather long. Perhaps there is a shorter route. Look here is one listed. It starts at Saskatchewan River Crossing and ends at Rocky Mountain House, but it is marked with a broken line. It's called Adventure Road," he pointed to the name. "Perhaps we could take this one. It seems to be shorter."

"We should ask at the information booth, if it is possible to drive this road. They will be able to tell us," I suggested.

Early next morning after breakfast we packed our gear, and drove to the information booth, which was located on the main road near the railroad station. The lady at the counter greeted us with a friendly smile and a, "good morning, what can I do for you?"

"We would like to drive this road," declared Kurt, pointing to the broken line on the map, "will that be possible?"

The lady studied the map and nodded in agreement. "It has not rained for six weeks and does not look as if it will for the next few days. I suppose it would be all right, but you must understand that this is not a paved or gravel road, only a dirt path, but if you drive carefully, you should get through."

"Well, let's try it," Kurt decided, "thus far Bonzo has behaved very well."

So began our memorable odyssey. On the way to Saskatchewan River Crossing we stopped at the Athabasca Falls, where the fast moving river races over rocks and through crevices falling approximately seventy feet to the depth. Andre was too daring for my motherly instincts, climbing to the edge of the fall.

"Andre, be careful, don't slip," I called out anxiously and Kurt added, "You'd better come back right now. We want to continue our drive because we still have a long way ahead of us."

We noticed several cars parked on the side of the road somewhere between Jasper and the Columbia Ice fields. Something brown was moving between the vehicles.

"It's a bear," I called out excitedly. Kurt pulled over to the side to stop Bonzo. People were taking photographs. We had barely come to a halt when the bear started to move towards our vehicle.

"Don't open the window," I cautioned our son. Our faces were pressed against the windowpanes. The animal stood up on its hind legs, looking at us through the glass hoping to be fed. He was a young bear of about two years of age. Suddenly he ran to the back and within a matter of seconds climbed up, sitting on top of the trailer. There he seemed to search frantically for something. His ascent was so sudden that it caught us off guard.

"What are we going to do? The bear will rip the tent to pieces. I have to get him off the trailer, "declared Kurt.

"Be careful," I warned. "The bear might charge."

"But we can't allow him to rip up the tent. I don't understand what he wants. I must try to entice him to jump down again."

"I still have some chocolates. Perhaps you will be able to do it with that," I suggested, as I looked for the sweets.

"Yes, that might do it," Kurt replied breaking off a piece of the chocolate, "but we must leave immediately, so he won't have a chance to climb back up again."

Kurt started the motor then opened the car door. Slowly, so as not to startle the bear, he walked towards the trailer trying to catch the animal's attention. The smell must have excited the bear. His beady little eyes followed Kurt's movements, as he threw the chocolate behind the trailer. Quickly the bear ran to the back to catch the piece of chocolate. Kurt in the meantime returned to his seat as fast as possible, slammed the door and threw in the forward gear. The vehicle sped forward. Looking through the rear window we could see the bear trailing behind for a short distance until he realized the futility of this undertaking and gave up the chase.

"I don't understand what the bear was looking for. There are only car parts and gasoline containers in the trailer," Kurt remarked throwing me a questioning look. Later at the next stop we discovered the answer to the puzzle. Before leaving the campground I had stashed a dishcloth in one of the trailer corners.

"It must have been the smell," Kurt said laughing as he held the dishcloth to his nose. "I must admit the bear has a damned good nose."

It was early afternoon when we arrived at Saskatchewan River Crossing. At that time the place had only a gas station and a small coffee shop. As soon as we had pulled up, the service station attendant stepped out. While he filled our Bonzo's tank, we asked him for directions. He looked a bit puzzled, then answered, "You'll have to turn left over there. The road is rather rough. I hope you know what you are doing."

"Yes, we have been told that it would be rough but possible."

We followed his directions turning onto a paved road. The pavement ended soon and a gravel road replaced it.

"That is not too bad," I declared triumphantly. "We should be in Rocky Mountain House within a few hours."

After about two miles the gravel road stopped. Two ruts continued from thereon. At some places the path had been washed out by melting water, but, although driving became more difficult, it was still possible to do so. Soon the path led into a densely wooded area. Dark firs and spruce grew close to the road their branches touching our vehicle at times. Heavy undergrowth would have prevented anyone to penetrate the forest further than about three feet. Tree trunks lay scattered about, some overgrown with moss, others splintered from lightning strikes. Except for Bonzo's motor purring like a contented kitten, we were surrounded by an eerie silence. The darkness was a little discomforting. There were no animals, not even a squirrel chattered. Between the treetops we could still get a glimpse of the towering mountain peaks high above.

"I hope we won't meet another car. I would be unable to get out of the way. There simply is not enough room for two vehicles," Kurt sighed worriedly.

Shortly thereafter a car did approach. Luckily at that point the path was a little wider so the two vehicles were able to squeeze by.

"See, other people have driven this road, so we should be able to do the same," Kurt remarked confidently.

At one point we discovered a green boarded up hunter's cabin. We stopped briefly to take a closer look. The door was barred with a heavy padlock, but it appeared, that nobody had been there for quite some time. We did not linger. After being on our way for about an hour, we arrived at a little creek. It was quite shallow.

"We'll be able to drive through it," Kurt commented self-assuredly slowly steering the vehicle through the approximately twelve inches high water.

"Piece of cake," he laughed, when he had safely reached the other side. The journey continued. Not long after we came to a second creek. This one, too, did not pose any serious problem for Bonzo. After we had conquered three more creeks, the sixth one looked ominous. It was approximately two feet in depth, and nine feet in width. The banks were rather steep. Rocks lay scattered throughout the riverbed. Milky glacier water was gushing over them. Kurt stopped Bonzo. We all stepped out. That was indeed an obstacle, which we had not anticipated. How could we safely reach the other side? With only a car it might have been possible to drive through without undue difficulties, but the trailer posed a considerable problem.

"How on earth will we manage that? I'm not sure that we will be able to get up on the other side with the trailer in tow. The bank is quite steep," pondered Kurt, staring at the water and stroking his chin, while contemplating a solution to the problem.

"Maybe we should unhitch the trailer and push it through by hand," I suggested.

"That would be impossible with the strong current. Furthermore the water is much too cold. We would get thoroughly soaked," he replied. "There must be another way."

"But what shall we do? It's too late to return to the highway. Soon it will be dark," I replied just as concerned and helpless.

"Perhaps I should back up a little so I'll have enough speed to get up on the other side," he declared finally.

"Do you think that this will work? Wouldn't it be better to go slow rather than fast," I replied not totally convinced that this approach was the answer.

"We might get stuck in the middle of the water. Then we would really be in trouble. We could not possibly push our heavy Bonzo up the slope. I think I should just try it."

I still had my doubts, but what did I know about driving cars? Kurt backed up a few feet. Then he put the car in forward gear, stepping so hard on the gas that the vehicle shot into the creek with great speed. Bonzo let out a groan, but Kurt managed to drive up on the other side with the trailer. As soon as we had crossed the creek and were safely on flat ground again, we noticed water spurting out from under Bonzo's hood. Kurt stopped and stepped out to open it. Then we saw the mess! Water gushed out with full force. The radiator had sprung a leak!!!

"Oh, for heaven's sake, what are we going to do now? The next service station is hours away. There is not a single soul out here, who will help us," I lamented. The case of my father's accident so many years ago shot through my mind. He had tried to pick up mother's family, who were unable to advance being stranded in a little village as they were fleeing from the advancing Russian Armies. The axle broke on his truck. It was minus 30 degrees Celsius. He had to make his way back on foot that time. Kurt also looked worried. Stroking his hair he stared helplessly at the mishap. Meanwhile the water gushed out.

"We might have been lucky. The break is fairly high," he finally declared. "I can clamp the heater cores together. There will be enough water running through the radiator to drive. We may have to stop frequently to let the motor cool down, but I'm sure Bonzo will take us home. Won't you, Bonzo? After all we really have no other choice," Kurt commented having recovered his composure. With a pair of pliers he squeezed the heater cores together. The water stopped squirting out, and we filled up the cooling system with creek water.

"Let's hope that it will hold together until we are home. It's high time that we get out of this

87

godforsaken no-man's-land. It will get dark quickly. I would like to be back on a proper road by then."

Fortunately, that had been the last creek. After a while we left the darkness of the forest entering an area, where the trees grew farther away from the path. Eventually light coloured poplars replaced the dark firs. The ruts became flatter, making it easier to drive. Through the trees on the right side of the path the blue-green water of Lake Abraham shimmered. The evening sun illuminated its still surface that it looked as if tiny diamonds splinters were dancing on it. The mountains in front of us were much lower than the Rockies, now looming at the rear.

"Oh, look what beautiful scenery!" I exclaimed excitedly. "What a wonderful view! Too bad we don't have a camera for taking coloured photos."

We had been driving uphill for a while. The ground became rocky and uneven. Deep below us was the lake. An almost vertical cliff rose on one side of the path and on the other a steep slope led straight down to the lake. Fearfully I stared at the abyss. A narrow curve now wound around the cliff. Andre, sitting in the back, asked me something. Turning my head I noticed to my horror that one of the wheels started to wobble. The trailer was already tilting dangerously towards the side of the lake.

"Kurt, stop the car. We are losing a wheel on the trailer!" I yelled in panic. He stopped at once. "That was lucky that you noticed it. Bonzo would have most likely been pulled down by the weight of the trailer. There might have been no stoppage. We must have had a guardian angel," he exclaimed, his face as white as a sheet. After recovering from the shock, he examined the wheel, pushing the trailer a little bit closer towards the hillside, and bracing it with a large stone.

"I've enough spare parts to repair it, but it'll take a while. You may as well walk around a little to stretch your legs."

Kurt started to work on the trailer, while Andre and I walked ahead on the path. The late afternoon sun illuminated the snow-covered peaks of the Rockies that they gleamed in a pink hue. The turquoise colour of the lake stood in stark contrast to the sandy coast on the other side. Wildflowers bloomed everywhere. An unreal silence enveloped the countryside, only a slight breeze fanned the leaves of the poplar trees, making a rustling noise. We noticed a few mountain goats climbing up the steep hill a short distance away, but as far as one could see, there was no sign of any human being or settlement. We were completely and utterly alone here.

After about half an hour the wheel was fastened to the trailer. We were able to continue on our calamitous journey.

"I sure hope that nothing else happens. Bonzo you must be a good boy. Take us home safely," Kurt said, stepping into the car and starting the motor. The lake beside the path seemed to stretch forever. Lower and lower the sun sank on the horizon. After a while the ruts disappeared. To our great relief we were finally driving on gravel road. Soon we reached the

Kootenay Plains. The landscape changed to hill country. Slowly the mighty mountains disappeared in the background. Seemingly endless coniferous forest stretched before us. After approximately two further hours the first fences and a few racing horses came into view. The worst was finally over. We breathed a sigh of relief.

"I believe we have reached the outskirts of civilization. There is still hope that we will eventually get home tonight."

Darkness crept up. Kurt had to turn on the headlights. Side roads branched off. Here and there houses appeared. It was almost midnight when we reached Rocky Mountain House. Andre had fallen asleep on the back seat, where all our bedding was piled up. Bonzo was thirsty, the tank almost empty. We drove through empty streets in search of an open gas station until we discovered a lit sign. Kurt pulled up to the pump. The service station attendant stepped out to fill the tank.

"Howdy folks. Where are you coming from so late at night?' he asked with a friendly tone of voice. "I was about to close up."

"Jasper," Kurt replied stretching his aching arms.

"But where do you want to drive to so late at night?"

"We have to get back to Edmonton because I have to work tomorrow."

"Don't tell me you drove the Adventure Road with this trailer?"

"Yes, we sure did."

"How did you make out? Did you run into difficulties? There are some rivers one must drive through."

"The radiator sprung a leak, we almost lost a wheel on the trailer, but otherwise we are still in one piece," Kurt laughed.

"Wouldn't' you better stay here overnight?" The man asked concerned then continued," we can fix your vehicle tomorrow."

"No, thank you, we have to get home."

"You still have quite a stretch to drive. It's a good three hours from here. Well, I wish you good luck. Get home safely," he remarked while counting the change.

"Thanks, we will best be driving on. It's getting late."

Kurt had a tough time staying awake. I had to make sure that he would not fall asleep at the wheel. Cruising along at a good speed on highway #2 just before reaching Edmonton, we suddenly heard police sirens and noticed red lights flashing. Kurt immediately pulled over and stopped, rolling down the window. The police car stopped in front of ours. An R.C.M.P. officer stepped out. Putting on his hat he walked to the driver's side window.

"Good evening, Sir, may I see your driver's license?" he asked politely.

"Certainly," Kurt answered then turned his head, "where is my wallet?"

"It must be in your jacket."

Kurt leaned over to the back searching for his jacket, which was buried beneath bedding and pieces of clothing. His hunting rifle lay on top of the mess. He lifted it up to move out of the way. It was not loaded, of course, but the policeman did not know that. He must have misinterpreted the gesture, because he slowly backed away from the vehicle. It struck me rather funny. I had to suppress a chuckle. We were much too tired to be posing a threat to anyone, especially to a police officer. In the meantime Kurt had found his jacket. He pulled out his driver's license, holding it out of the window.

"Here it is, Sir."

Cautiously the policeman returned to the vehicle. He seemed to be still unsure if any danger was lurking in the darkness. But he took the driver's license, examining it and was obviously satisfied. With his flashlight he shone inside the car, where he discovered our son asleep on the back seat.

"May I ask where you are coming from?" he inquired politely.

"We are on our way home from Jasper. Did I drive too fast?" Kurt inquired a bit concerned.

"No, but one of the trailer lights is burned out," the officer replied.

"I'm sorry, I hadn't noticed it. The wires must have become disconnected when the wheel came off."

"Where did that happen?"

"On the Adventure Road," Kurt responded.

"On the Adventure Road? You drove from Jasper over the Adventure Road with this trailer?"

"Yes, Sir."

"That is a dangerous road. I drove it once. You are lucky that you didn't come to any harm. Well, you would better drive home without delay to get some sleep. You must be very tired. I will not write you a ticket, but you need to have the problem fixed as soon as possible."

"Yes, Sir, thank you. I promise I will look after it tomorrow."

We finally reached our home after three o'clock in the morning.

"It'll be a short night," Kurt sighed, "but despite all the mishaps I have enjoyed the trip."

"I wouldn't have wanted to miss it for anything in the world," I replied yawning. "It was indeed an adventure."

A brand new highway, the David Thompson, was built a few years later. Today one can reach Rocky

93

Mountain House from Saskatchewan River Crossing within about three hours' time. The highway closely follows the path of the old Adventure Road, except for the part, where the travelers had to drive through six creeks. The remnants of the old road have almost all disappeared. Sometimes, when we drive the David Thompson on our way to and from British Columbia, Jasper or Banff, we stop to look up to the cliff high above the present highway. The curve is still visible to the trained eye, where many, many years ago we almost lost our lives on that fateful journey.

18. THE RED SHOES

A pair of red shoes on display in a show window had caught my attention. They had high heels, and were made of real leather. Every time I passed the shoe store, I admired the beautiful shoes. I wanted so much to own then. One lunch hour, I finally went into the shoe store to ask for the price.

"These are $16.00," the clerk answered. "They are made in Germany."

They looked so elegant, so tempting, but it was a lot of money to pay when a good pair of leather shoes cost about $3.50 in those years. I would have to think about it. Half my life I had, for lack of available merchandize, worn used shoes, hand-me-downs, which did not fit very well. They were mostly too small squeezing my toes. Later, when shoes became available, I had to buy sturdy leather shoes for daily use because they had to last a long time. High heeled shoes were used only for going out and not suitable for every day. I didn't miss them until now, because we didn't go out very often, but the situation had changed. There were occasions when we were invited and I wanted to look presentable. But spending $16.00 wasn't that a bit too extravagant? That money would be needed for more important purchases. On the other hand it would be nice if I could dress up for special occasions. Debating with myself I went home.

"Why don't you buy them?" Kurt said after I told him about the shoes. "If you like them so much then what is stopping you?"

"But it's so much money, which we need for other things," I argued.

"We'll get over it. You haven't had anything new for a long time."

The next day I went to the store and tried them on. They fitted perfectly, but to my surprise they were a size larger than I usually needed. Funny, I knew exactly my shoe size, and these were made in Germany so they should be the correct size. Perhaps they had changed the shoe sizes, or they made them smaller for export. Whatever the reason, I gave it no further thought and bought the red shoes. They looked gorgeous and fitted like a glove. I was in my glory feeling like a queen. Speaking of a queen, *Queen Elizabeth II* was coming to visit Edmonton in July of 1959. That was only a few days away. I had promised Andre to take him downtown to see our monarch. It would be an occasion to wear the red shoes.

The next day I developed a rash all over my body. The itch drove me crazy. I went to see the doctor, who gave me an injection, an antidote for allergies.

"What did you do? Did you take any medication?" he asked.

"I had a sore throat and there was a penicillin pill left from Andre's throat infection, so I took it."

"You should never take penicillin without a doctor's prescription," he scolded.

"But I had penicillin before," I argued.

"You can develop an allergy at any time, so don't do that again. If you feel bad or have any other symptoms, come back immediately," he advised and shaking my hand opened the door.

The same evening I stripped and changed all the bed linen, throwing the soiled ones into a tub of water to soak overnight. Tomorrow was wash day. I still had to scrub everything by hand on a wash board. We had no washing machine as yet, but we had a car!

In the middle of the night I awoke with a burning thirst. I left the bed and went to the kitchen to get a glass of water. The next thing I remember was looking up into Kurt's face.

"You must have fainted," he said helping me get up. My body was covered with a rash. I felt lousy.

"I'll call an ambulance," he said.

"Please don't, I'll be all right. I have to wash clothes today," I protested, but he wouldn't listen. A few minutes later the ambulance arrived with blaring sirens. After loading me onto a stretcher and shoving me into the vehicle, the ambulance drove out of our driveway. The sirens howled all the way to the hospital. Their roaring sound reverberated inside the vehicle, which was very annoying.

What happened after admission is a little blurred in my mind, but I vaguely remember a great number of doctors congregating around my bed and discussing things. My case must have been a sensation, something many doctors had not seen. Penicillin allergies were not as common as they are today. My body was swelling up like a balloon. The itch was unbearable. A nurse brought a bottle of Calamine lotion and smeared the liquid all over my body. I looked like a pink elephant, but it eased the itch. The swelling became worse during the next night. Soon I could not open my eyes anymore; they were completely shut. I could feel how my tongue became enlarged and breathing was difficult.

My girlfriend came to visit me the day after admission and promptly walked out of the room, because she did not recognize my distorted face. I must have looked hideous. All orifices were swollen shut.

But I guess it was not my time yet to die. I survived the ordeal. After a week Kurt was told to bring the largest dress he could find to take me home. He brought me a wide skirt, but I still could not close the zipper on it. My circumference must have been at least three inches larger than normal.

A surprise was waiting for me at home. A washing machine stood in the kitchen!!!

The doctors had told Kurt that I might not survive. He had no choice but take care of the wash himself. Not knowing what to do, he went out and bought a washing machine on credit. (*It is amazing how fast helpful household machinery appears, when men have to do the work.*) My friend and neighbour, Dorothy, had cleaned my house in the meantime and taken care of Andre. Unfortunately our son did not see the queen when she came to visit Edmonton.

Slowly my body began to look normal again. The swelling disappeared, but, when I tried to put on my new red shoes, I discovered to my utter disgust that they were about an inch too long and wide.   Oh, my beautiful new shoes.   All that money I had spent went down the drain. My dream of looking desirable like a lady vanished into thin air. But I could not possibly throw these expensive shoes away, so I stuffed the toes part with Kleenex and glued a little cushion into the back. It still was uncomfortable walking in them, but I managed. Eventually they wore out and were thrown away. Perhaps it was a lesson I had to learn about vanity.

19. BUYING A HOUSE.

It was definitely more enjoyable living in a house than an apartment. The urge to own one became stronger and stronger. We began looking at ads and finally contacted a real estate agent.

"I can't see how we can come up with a down payment," Kurt mentioned one day. "We would need at least $500.00.

"I've saved up enough from the household money and together with the money we have in the bank we should be able to swing it," I replied. He looked at me shocked. "How were you able to hide that from me?"

"If I had told you, it would have been gone. There is always something that is needed or wanted, and if the money is not there, you don't miss whatever was so urgent."

The real estate agent had found an old house for sale. It stood close to the street. Kurt looked at it. "I could build a proper house at the back. There is enough room there. We could live in this place until the new one is finished. Then we can pull the old one down."

The house was a white wooden structure. Window frames were painted in black. It had three very small rooms and a kitchen. There was also a toilet inside. The bathtub was in the dug-out basement next to the furnace. It looked a bit ramshackle and crooked. We decided to buy it for the asking price of $6,000.00. At that time we had no idea that one had to bargain for a lower price, being used to paying what was asked.

First own house

The first of March, 1960, the day we were moving, was bitter cold. The thermometer showed thirty degrees below in Fahrenheit. Upon entering the place we discovered that it was left in very dirty condition with a pile of garbage on the kitchen floor and a pail of dirty diapers. I had my work cut out cleaning the old place and the new one. But I didn't mind the extra work. It was a wonderful feeling to finally have our own domicile, where nobody could give us orders or tell us what to do or not to do. For the next few weeks I was in my glory, decorating and painting. The house became a home within a short period of time. It didn't look much from the outside, but one got a warm feeling inside.

During the winter we had a number of visitors under our roof. A family of sparrows had taken up residence there. There was a constant chirping and chattering above our kitchen ceiling.

Kurt's job was secure and I had found a new one working for a German physician, who had advertised for a German speaking receptionist. I had attended a typing course in the meantime and was able to type letters, but I must confess that my typing speed left something to be desired. Nevertheless I was hired.

The next spring Kurt decided to start with the necessary paper work for building the new house. He went to City Hall trying to obtain permission for building the place. To his great disappointment he was told that the zoning law for that area had been changed. New houses had to be built not more than a certain distance from the front. This made it impossible to comply with the law unless we pulled down the existing home.

"We won't be able to build the new house here. The measurements won't fit. We would have to move out. In order to build the new place, the old one would have to go," he said coming home in a bleak mood.

"That is really too bad. We'll have to save up more money and then sell this place and buy another one," I replied. And so we started saving again.

20. THE SKI TRIP

It seemed such a long time since we had skied for the last time in the Giant Mountains. There was so much snow in Canada that the temptation to go skiing became irresistible.

On Christmas Eve we were all in a festive mood. Ornaments, glittering in the artificial lights, hung from the branches of the lovingly decorated Christmas tree. Throughout the house drifted the sweet aroma of spice cookies. A bowl filled with nuts and sweets stood on the table. Under the tree lay brand new wooden skis, poles and boots for everyone. I was elated about the presents, but Andre, nine years old by now, did not hide his disappointment. He had never skied before. At his age it was understandable that he was not enthusiastic about the planned trip.

We went to bed early on Christmas Eve intending to rise at four o'clock in the morning to be in Jasper when the lift opened. Driving to Jasper the night before and staying at a motel would have been more convenient, but money was still in short supply.

The alarm clock rang much too early the next morning. Still sleepy and yawning we marched one after the other to the bathroom.

"Hurry up, we have to leave," I shouted to Andre, who sat on his bed with a grumpy face putting on his heavy winter clothing. "I don't want to go," he mumbled. "Why don't we stay home?"

"Oh, stop complaining. I'm sure you'll enjoy the trip. Just wait until you stand on top of the mountain. It is a beautiful sight from there. You'll have a lot of fun," I encouraged him, but his bad mood did not improve.

After a quick breakfast, we fastened the ski equipment on top of the vehicle and left. I was driving the first stretch from Edmonton to Edson. Having recently obtained my driver's licence I was eager to use my newly acquired skill. It was still dark outside; no light shone from the windows. Shortly after leaving the city, Kurt and Andre fell asleep. Andre lay curled up on the back seat. Kurt was sitting beside me with his head leaning back. Nowhere was a vehicle on the road during those early morning hours. Our old Bonzo's headlights threw their yellow beams onto a seemingly endless straight road. Poplars stretched their empty branches into the air like ghostly apparitions in an otherwise white winter landscape. A coyote ran across the highway, but quickly disappeared in the bushes beside the road. Once in a while there were Christmas lights lit on a lonely farmhouse. It was a pleasant distraction during this boring drive. Not a single headlight beam from an oncoming vehicle broke the blackness of night forcing me to stay alert. I had already passed the small towns of Entwistle and Wildwood, also Chip Lake. Driving became rather tiring. No one talked to me. There was no radio reception. The curves before Edson wound from one side to the other. It started to snow now. Heavy flakes whirled in the air, and the windshield wipers waved monotonously back and forth. The hum of the motor was lulling. It was so comfortably warm inside the vehicle. Heavier and heavier the lids became …heavier and…

"Stop the car immediately and get out," Kurt suddenly yelled rudely awakening my senses. He yanked the steering wheel from my hand, pushed my

103

foot off the gas pedal and stepped on the brakes so hard that the car came to an abrupt halt.

"Do you want us to get killed" he screamed. "If I hadn't woken up who knows where we would have ended up. Your head was already drooping onto the steering wheel." Then he added a little more gently, "why didn't you wake me when you were too tired to drive? I could have taken the wheel."

Bitter cold air hit my face as soon as I opened the door. I was awake immediately.

"Walk around the vehicle a few times," Kurt ordered. I gladly obeyed.

"Now I can drive again. I'm fully awake," I offered.

"Oh, no, you don't. You are much too tired. I won't take any more chances," he replied passionately moving over to the driver's seat. I had to admit to myself that it was the right decision, because the tiredness was overwhelming.

It was still pitch black outside when we reached Edson. All inhabitants of the little town seemed to be asleep. Nowhere did we see a single soul and no light escaped from any of the windows.

"I'm going to fill up," my husband announced. "It'll be more expensive in Jasper."

He drove through the silent streets in search of an open gas station, but everything was closed.

104

"The owners must have an agreement with the Hinton gas stations. They are probably taking turns staying open for Christmas," he mumbled finally. "There is enough gas in the tank to get us there. Something must be open."

Without giving it another thought we continued our drive. It was about seven o'clock in the morning and still dark when we reached Hinton. Here, too, we were unable to discover any lit gas station signs. Everything was closed, not even a coffee shop was open. After driving around the town for a while we gave up the search.

"Perhaps we can get gas at the Park entrance," I said hopefully.

"I doubt that they are selling gas, but perhaps they will be good enough to siphon some from their own tanks, so we'll at least reach Jasper. We just have to try it. What other choice do we have?" he replied.

The booth at the park gate was completely deserted. Not a single soul was anywhere to be seen. Everything was locked.

"We wouldn't have to pay park fee today, if we had no sticker," Kurt laughed driving through the open gate. But I became panicky. "How much gas is there still left in the tank?" I asked.

"It's almost empty. I don't think we'll reach Jasper with it," he answered looking at the gauge worriedly. "It's approximately forty miles from here,

105

but it's of no use waiting. Who knows when they will open up today, perhaps not at all?"

We did not speak for a while silently praying for a miracle. The little wooden cabins at the motel in Pocahontas were buried in snow up to the windowsills. There was no sign of life anywhere.

"I've an idea," Kurt suddenly said. "The camping stove is still in the trunk. There must be some fuel left in the container. It's not the right stuff, but if I put it into the gas tank it will mix with what is left of the gasoline. That might just do the trick."

"Won't it damage the motor?"

"It is not recommended, but certainly better than taking the chance of freezing to death on Christmas Day," he declared while he stopped Bonzo. An icy wind blew in his face as he opened the trunk. The temperature was dropping steadily.

"Yes, there is some gas left. It should be enough to get us to Jasper," he commented, pouring the camping stove fuel into the tank.

The problem was successfully resolved for now, as the motor ran on the mixture. Actually it was running quite smoothly. Our sense of humor returned. Slowly the darkness began to lift. A leaden, grey winter morning dawned. Soon the surrounding area became more recognizable. Moisture-laden clouds hung in the sky. The peaks of the Rockies were covered with snow. From the distance they appeared in a purplish-blue hue interrupted by the dark, greyish-blue of the coniferous forest. Now the triangular shaped dome of Pyramid Mountain came into view. We traveled along the frozen Talbot Lake, which looked as if a white woolen blanket was spread over it. On the hills, where the wind had swept the snow away, bushels of brown grass poked through. Here and there deer, elk and a herd of mountain sheep nibbled on the meager feed.

Approximately a mile before Jasper the last drop in the gas tank was used up. The motor died.

"What are we going to do now?" I sighed looking helpless at the snow-covered road in front of us.

"We'll have to push," Kurt answered. "We can't sit here and wait for help. Without the motor running there will be no heat in the car and we would freeze to death. It's obvious that nobody is driving today. We haven't met a single car during the entire morning. Get out and start pushing. It's not too far anymore."

With one hand on the steering wheel and Andre and I at the back we all began to push our heavy Bonzo. The temperature was still dropping. Our fingers became cold and stiff despite the heavy mittens. Soon we had no feeling in them. Kurt urged us along. We pushed – and pushed – until finally the first houses of Jasper came into view.

"Let's stop here for a moment that we can all catch our breath," I whined exhausted.

"My hands are so cold. I can't go on," Andre lamented. "I didn't want to go skiing. Now see what happened."

"Stop complaining," I called angrily. "How could we possibly know that nothing is open today?"

"O.k., let's stop for a while, but then we have to continue otherwise the cold will be getting the best of us," Kurt finally gave in. After one or two minutes we realized ourselves that we had to push in order to keep warm. It was a blessing that the road to Jasper was still straight in those years not like today where it goes uphill just before entering. With our last strength we shoved the car along the main street of Jasper, and parked it in front of the Astoria Hotel.

"We'll go inside to warm up, and then we'll need to find someone who is willing to sell us gas," Kurt declared as we climbed up the few steps to the lobby. It felt wonderful when the heat in the foyer hit our faces. With a sigh of relief we dropped onto the chairs standing there. Kurt looked around, but there was nobody, neither at the desk nor in the dining room or kitchen.

"Funny, the people must be still asleep. It's nine o'clock already. Where is everybody?"

After a short while we heard footsteps. '*Papa Andrews*', the hotel proprietor descended the stairs. He looked very sleepy and unkempt wearing a housecoat and slippers.

"Where on earth are you folks coming from? It's so early still," he called out dumbfounded while yawning. "You look as if you ran into trouble. Is there anything I can do for you?"

"We came from Edmonton to go skiing, but ran out of gas on the way. Neither in Edson nor Hinton was a service station open. We had to push the car the last mile," Kurt explained.

"But today is Christmas! Nobody works on Christmas! The ski lift won't be open today," he instructed us, while shaking his head in disbelief. How stupid could these greenhorns be? But when he realized our disappointment, he added, "Don't get all upset. I'll help you. Go to the dining room to warm up. As soon as I have everything organized, I will bring you coffee and breakfast. Just give me a few minutes. My chef has the day off. I must do it myself. Then I will also see to it that you get gas."

We rid ourselves of coats, mittens and toques, and dropped onto the chairs at the dining table. The room was festively decorated. A Christmas tree stood in one corner. Papa Andrews turned on the artificial lights. Music sounded from somewhere. Then he stoked the embers in the fireplace that the flames shot up spreading comfortable warmth. Afterwards he disappeared in the kitchen. Soon the delicious odour of freshly brewed coffee drifted in. Carrying a tray he placed a hearty breakfast of toast and eggs on the table.

"Dig in," he said with a friendly smile.

We did not need an invitation. Slowly the sensation in our fingers returned. We felt human again. Then we heard Papa Andrews talk to someone on the telephone in the other room. "Get your arse out of bed and open up the pump," he hollered into the receiver. "These people need gas and you'll sell it to them. So it is Christmas. I don't care if it is. They are unable to go on. I'll send them over in about half an hour."

We heard him hang up the receiver. Then he returned to the dining room with a broad smile.

"He's going to sell you gas, but first eat breakfast. You'll have lots of time today."

After we paid Papa Andrews and thanked him for his help and kindness he showed us the service station, which was located only a few houses down the road.

"Why are you in Jasper today?" asked the gas station owner while filling the tank.

"We wanted to go skiing, but, as we have been told already, the lift is closed today because nobody works on Christmas."

"Sorry you are out of luck, but everything will be working again tomorrow."

We thanked the man for opening up the service station especially for us, and paid the bill. Finally we were mobile again. As we turned the next corner at the end of the main street we noticed two people, who

110

were pushing a Volkswagen. They looked very familiar to us.

"Isn't that Wilfried and his fiancée?" asked Kurt pointing to the couple.

It really was my brother and his girl, who struggled pushing the little Volkswagen through the deep snow.

"What are you doing here?" we asked as soon as we reached them.

"We wanted to go skiing, but couldn't get any gas," they answered. "There was no gas station open anywhere."

"Yes, we discovered that too, and had to push Bonzo the last mile. Papa Andrews arranged that one gas station has opened up for us. It's over there. If you hurry, the owner will still be there," we advised them, then helped push their vehicle to the service station.

The temperature had dropped to about fifteen degrees below zero, but now the sun was peeking through the clouds. Everything looked a lot friendlier knowing that nothing could happen anymore since the tank was full of gas. We had reserved a motel room for the coming night already and decided to check in.

"We'll play cards. I've brought a deck," Wilfried suggested.

And so we spent Christmas Day in the motel playing cards. In the late afternoon we ventured to the empty dining room, where the owner served us a self-prepared meal. His chef was away too, as nobody worked on Christmas Day. We were his only guests. After we had finished our meal, he came to the table to sit with us for a little chat, inquiring as to where we came from and how we liked Canada. Then he told us a few things about the history of Jasper. Afterwards he went back to the kitchen only to return with a crafty smile and a bottle of brandy, some of which he poured into our coffee cups.

"I'm not allowed to sell liquor, but, if you promise not to tell anyone, I'll give it to you as a Christmas present," he said holding his index finger over his mouth. His blue eyes sparkled roguishly like that of a little boy who has gotten into mischief.

At that time it was prohibited to sell liquor, except in government liquor stores. Never before or since has anyone served us brandy in a coffee mug, but we nevertheless enjoyed the drink. Years later we still remembered the kind host, who had tried to restore the Christmas spirit upon the disappointed travelers.

The ski-lift opened the next day, the temperature rose, and we skied until early afternoon. Exhausted from the unaccustomed, physical exercise, but happy and content we drove home without experiencing any more unexpected fiascos.

Although the trip had caused us some tense moments and frightening hours, it also left us with fond memories, especially the helpfulness of *Papa Andrews* and the owners of the motel and gas station.

Very few people, mostly immigrants from Europe, skied at Jasper's Marmot Basin or Whistler's Mountain during those early years, as the ski sport was not as widely practiced as today. The sleepy town of Jasper has changed into a bustling tourist resort in the meantime, and the ski area has chair lifts. A large chalet with all amenities was erected on the mountain. Since the Yellowhead highway was built, the service stations in Edson and Hinton are open, even on Christmas Day!

21. MOTHER'S VISIT

Five years had passed since we left Germany. It seemed such a long time already since I had last seen my parents. I missed them very much and longed to embrace at least one of them. The only communication was by mail or telephone. Telephone calls were very expensive during those early years, so we only phoned after midnight when the rates were lower. They also had to be very short so as not to waste any precious minute. At that time a call to Germany cost $10.00 for three minutes. It was a luxury we seldom could afford.

We debated who we should invite to come first, as we only had enough money to pay for one ticket. Our father was in ill health. It probably wouldn't be advisable for him to undertake such a long journey right now. It would have cost a fortune, if our father had become very ill here or died. Therefore it was decided to have our mother come first. Our parents had been living on welfare for the past few years due to Father's illness. Our mother earned a few marks with housecleaning, but that was not nearly enough to pay for a trip to Canada. Father had applied for a pension, but so far this had not been granted.

Our mother arrived in early June after a disastrous sea journey. The boat, she had been travelling on, was caught in a severe storm. One of the ship's engines was damaged. A new one had to be installed at sea, which delayed the arrival by a few days. Mother was seasick during the entire voyage. She stated upon her arrival in Edmonton that she would rather die than have to set foot on a ship again.

It was an emotional greeting when we picked her up at the railway station. Tears of joy were rolling down my cheeks. After we drove home there was so much to show and talk about that we stayed up until long past midnight. She told us about the many changes that had taken place since we left Bremerhaven. The economy had started to pick up in Germany, new houses were being built and businesses flourished.

Two days after arrival her suitcase had not been delivered yet by the Canadian National Railway. We worried that it might be lost and phoned, but were told that it was not there. Mother had to borrow some of my clothes, which was rather inconvenient, as they did not fit properly. Kurt finally drove Mother to the railway station. A nice gentleman walked with them through the premises. In an empty hall somewhere in the basement they discovered Mother's suitcase. It

114

stood there all alone. Perhaps it had been forgotten or was misplaced. Luckily nothing was missing.

A drive to Jasper was planned for the next week end. The weather was already warm enough for camping. We gathered all our camping gear, tent, bedding, pots and pans and camp stove. Mother needed a pair of long pants. She protested vehemently about such a purchase, telling us that she could not possibly wear long pants. It simply was not ladylike. What would her sisters in Germany think of her? We had to convince her that this was the only way to go camping. *She had not seen our wilderness yet, having the same misconception as I had when we went to the lake for the first time.* We suggested that she could leave the pants here when she returned home, and not tell her sisters about them. Satisfied with this solution she finally agreed to our suggestion.

On Saturday morning we packed up our old Bonzo and started the drive. We had not come very far, not even to Spruce Grove, when Bonzo suddenly stopped. He lay down on the highway tired and worn out from the endless miles he had driven. No amount of coaxing made him move an inch. Kurt tried every trick he knew, but it was to no avail. I guess Bonzo died of old age.

"What are we going to do now?" I called out.

"You can stay in the car. I'll walk to the nearest telephone and call a tow truck. Perhaps I can catch a ride," Kurt said, and set out on foot for the long trek.

It took quite a while until the tow truck arrived. The driver loaded up Bonzo, and then drove us to a bus stop from where we could get home. Bonzo was towed to the graveyard for cars, the auto wreckers. It was indeed a sad day when we had to say good bye to our beloved Bonzo. It felt as if a member of the family had passed away. He had always brought us home safely. We remembered the wonderful trips to the mountains, the excitement of seeing so many new things, the wild animals and the experience of being in the great outdoors. Life would have been dull without him. It might have taken years before we saw the breathtaking beauty of the Canadian Rockies, if it hadn't been for our Bonzo.

"We'll have to buy a car. I can't get to work with the bus. It would take me hours," Kurt finally said while contemplating how we would manage our money. "We'll have to buy it on credit. There is no other way."

The next day we went on a car buying tour. Our old neighbour and friend, Irving, drove us to the dealer, where we chose a brand new Ford Galaxie. With a new car nothing would go wrong anymore, as it was on warranty, or would it? A few months later we discovered the truth. That new vehicle was not as reliable as our old Bonzo, but that is another story. We didn't give the new car a nickname and simply called it the Galaxie. Next week end we would be driving to the mountains no matter what! Nothing would stop us this time. Mother was anxious to see them, having heard so much about their beauty already.

116

Andre and Helga with new Galaxie

It was early in the morning. I was just getting ready to go to work when the telegram arrived. It read: *Father passed away this morning. Please come home.*

Our mother had been here for barely two weeks. It was as if a bomb had hit. Although our father had been in ill health for the past ten years, nobody had expected anything drastic to happen.

Our brother, Reinhard, was still too young to care for our father, so Mother had asked one of our oldest employees, Mrs. Bergmann, to stay with them until she returned. In the olden days, when we still had our business, Mrs. Bergmann had been like a member of the family. She was with the company for over thirty years. That morning Mrs. Bergmann had discovered our father lying on his bed. It seemed that he had tried to get up and collapsed.

Although the ship's passage had been paid for our mother already, other arrangements needed to be made now. It would have taken much too long to return home in time for the funeral via sea voyage. We phoned the travel agent, trying to arrange a quick return trip to Germany. It was not easy to find a flight with an empty seat, because most seats were booked months in advance. The travel agent was very helpful phoning around. Two hours later the phone rang.

"We have a seat booked for your mother, but she'll have to leave this afternoon." The lady at the travel agency advised. We would have to pay an extra fee, but the missed ship's passage was to be credited. Our mother was spared the much feared boat ride home. She arrived before funeral arrangements were made.

After my mother's departure the realization that I would never see my father again set in with a vengeance. He had been my idol, a patient man, who provided me with love and nurturing. He had always been there when I needed him. I fondly remembered the many times before the war when he drove to the Giant Mountains, and walked with us to the highest peak, the Snow Cap. There were the potato fires on the field in front of the factory, when all friends and family were invited, and the sleigh rides and company outings with horses and wagons. In my mind I can still see him standing on the ramp in front of the factory entrance, holding a cigar in one hand and giving instructions to the workers.

This trip must have started under the auspices of a bad star, because everything seemed to go wrong. It was unfortunate, but to make up for all inconveniences and upsets, a higher power later granted our mother numerous journeys to Canada by plane, and many camping trips to the Rocky Mountains, Yellowstone Park and Alaska.

It was rather ironic that Father's pension was finally granted a week before his death.

22. THE EASTER WEEKEND

Winter storms swept over the vast, endless prairie like rabid dogs, burying the land under a heavy blanket of snow. Once in a while the thermometer dropped to minus 40 degrees Fahrenheit in the city, and even lower in the surrounding countryside. Icicles hung from some of the eaves. Chimneys emitted smoke continuously. Ice crystals painted the most intricate patterns on windowpanes. Brownish sleet piled up in the streets forming ruts and making driving difficult. Most people looked pale and tired, having spent endless hours indoors. Men and beast were yearning for the return of the warm days of summer.

Finally the temperature began to rise. During the first week of April a warm spell melted the remaining snow. Pussy willows started to bloom and tulip sprouts broke through the hard earth. A few days ago the first flock of wild geese flew in perfect V formation over the city, returning from their winter quarters in the south. It was a sure sign that spring was just around the corner.

"Let's go skiing on Easter," Wilfried suggested, as we were playing cards one evening. "If it stays that warm, there soon won't be much snow left."

"We don't have enough money to pay for a hotel room and the lift tickets," I sighed, downheartedly.

"We could sleep in the tent. The ground should be dry enough. You have bought that big tent and the camping stove recently. That should be sufficient. Why don't we try it?" Wilfried suggested confidently.

"You must be joking. Camping in April? I've never heard of anything so silly." I laughed, not taking him serious, but Kurt thought about it for a while, and then agreed with Wilfried.

"If we take enough warm blankets along, it will be all right. In case it's getting too cold during the night, we can still check into a motel. Perhaps we should risk it."

Skiing was our favourite winter sport, but we could not afford to drive to the mountains very often, and stay at a hotel overnight. The price of the ski lift tickets and the additional gas and food cost were enough to throw our budget off balance. Camping would certainly be the ideal solution, but I shivered just thinking of the cold nights in the tent.

"Well, if you believe that we won't get too cold, perhaps we should give it a try." I finally agreed not wanting to spoil their enthusiasm.

"I'll bring a few friends. It will keep us warm sleeping close together," Wilfried added with a grin.

"We'll meet you at Wapiti campground on Good Friday."

On Friday morning we left the city. In the ink blue Alberta-sky hung a scorching sun promising perfect weather for skiing. After the seemingly never ending winter months, we would be able to soak up the heat, and perhaps come home with an incredible suntan much to the envy of our co-workers.

In the early afternoon we arrived at the Wapiti campground in Jasper, but discovered to our dismay that it was closed. That possibility had never crossed our minds. Needless to say we were disappointed.

"The overflow area at Wabasso might be open," Kurt said.

"I hope we won't miss Wilfried and his friends," I replied, but Kurt shook his head replying confidently," I'm sure we'll find them. They'll be somewhere. Jasper isn't a big city."

A chain hung at the entrance to the Wabasso overflow area with a sign 'closed'. We looked at each other dumbfounded. Perhaps we would have to stay in a hotel after all. Secretly I hoped for the possibility. The camping solution did not suit me, but I kept the thought to myself.

"There is a picnic area with tables, benches and an outhouse a few miles from here. That is all we need."

"But it's so far from Jasper. Wilfried won't find us out there," I muttered.

"We'll just have to drive back to Jasper. He must be somewhere."

There was no snow on the ground in the vicinity of Jasper. Only here and there at shady spots, where the sun rays had not penetrated the ground, a few patches survived. The whistling of marmots caught our attention. We discovered their little heads poking out of holes in a meadow. Wapitis grazed at a hillside adjacent to the highway. Birds twittered. Everywhere one felt the joy of awakening life. New growth returned to the barren landscape. Soon the first green shoots would paint the forest in a soft shade of green. The bears would leave their dens, and mother bears roam the woods with their cubs, venturing down to the highway to beg for food. Finally winter was hiding its ugly face. In a few weeks the snow would also melt on the mountains and ski season come to an end.

Suddenly Kurt called out," Look, there is Wilfried with his friends."

A group of young people, among them my brother, walked in the middle of the road unconcerned of the danger of approaching vehicles, as there was no traffic on the old highway #93 to Banff at that time of year. Kurt had to step sharply on the brakes to avoid them. It occurred in a bend, where the road was rather steep. Brakes squealed. The car stopped abruptly. With a loud, screeching noise the wooden box on top of the vehicle, in which we had stowed our luggage, slid down, landing in front of the young people, who scattered to the sides. We stepped out to look at the mishap. Luckily no one was hurt. The boys helped Kurt lift up the box and secure it safely on the roof.

"Where did you come from?" we asked.

"We left both Volkswagens at the picnic area and went for a walk hoping to meet up with you, but it was not necessary to greet us with such force," Wilfried laughed.

"Hop in. I'll give you a lift to the picnic area. You can help me pitch the tent. It is very heavy. A few more hands will make it easier," Kurt suggested. Wilfried shook his head and replied, "No, we'll walk back. Wait a few minutes until we arrive. We'll help you set up the tent."

Pitching the tent was quickly accomplished. The girls helped me set the table and prepare some food.

"We'll need water. The tap is not yet open. We only brought enough for drinking and cooking."

"I'll go down to the river and hack a hole into the ice. Mathew and Gordon you come along. We'll use the river water for washing the dishes and ourselves. The water in the container is for drinking and cooking only."

Wilfried searched the trunk for an axe. As soon as he had found one, the boys went to the nearby Athabasca River opposite the picnic place. They hacked an opening into the ice, filled up some containers, and returned them.

"Let's drive back to Jasper and take a look at the lakes," Wilfried suggested. "It's too early to crawl into bed."

"O.k., good idea," we all agreed.

We returned to Jasper, crossed the river and drove to Lake Edith. Having arrived at the lakeshore, we sat on the park benches to relax in the warm evening sun. A squirrel chattered, but otherwise everything was silent. The cabins on the other side of the lake were still boarded up, as the owners had not yet retuned. Wilfried and his friends could not resist the temptation of walking on the ice, which still covered the lake.

"Don't go too far," we called after them worried that they may break through the ice. It seemed still thick enough, but how much had melted underneath was anyone's guess.

Finally they returned safely to the shore, except for Wilfried, who was still jumping on the ice, trying to find out if it would crack. We watched his foolishness, wondering what he was trying to prove. He was tempting the patience of the universe with his daring spirit.

"Come back," I called out worried. "Are you crazy? You are too heavy for such nonsense. You'll break through the ice."

It was only a moment later that the mishap occurred. We could hear the ice crack. Then he plunged into the frigid waters of Lake Edith. Everything happened in the blink of an eye. Everyone was taken by surprise. Luckily the breakthrough occurred not far from the shore where the water was shallow. Wilfried was able to climb out of the water quickly. However, after returning to shore, he turned his pockets inside out searching for his wallet only to discover that it had disappeared together with his car keys.

"I lost my wallet!" he called out in despair. We didn't believe our eyes, when we saw him run back and jump into the icy waters again, frantically searching for his wallet. It was sheer madness. His head popped underneath the ice. We feared that he would drown because of the cold. But then suddenly he climbed out of the water.

"I found it!" he yelled triumphantly, holding up the wallet. His body was shaking like a leaf, his lips were bluish tinged, and his face was ghostly white.

"We have to find him some dry clothes," I urged, "or he will end up with pneumonia or God knows what."

Unfortunately we had neither blankets nor dry clothes in the car, as everything had been left inside the tent. The boys decided that each one would take off a piece of clothing. One boy handed him his pants, another one his undershirt and yet another one his sweater. One of the girls took off her socks. We found a toque and some mittens in the car. Wilfried had to strip completely to put on the dry clothes. Most of the items were too small for him, except for the sweater, which was rather large, but everything was dry.

Despite driving as fast as possible, we needed more than half an hour for our return trip to camp. Upon arrival Kurt quickly lit the camp stove inside the tent. Wilfried put on fresh underwear and returned the borrowed clothes. Unfortunately, the ski pants, ski jacket and socks were the only spare clothes he had brought along. The wet ones were hung up on a clothesline inside the tent to dry, but leather pants and shoes needed several days. He would have to wear his ski outfit for the remainder of the trip.

The sun quickly disappeared behind the mountains. With approaching darkness the temperature dropped. We heated up a pot of soup on the camp stove for supper and then crawled into our sleeping bags.

Next morning Wilfried was all right. He didn't suffer any ill effects from his unexpected plunge into the icy lake, and so we went out to ski. People had to park their cars at a designated area at the bottom of the road to Marmot Basin. At that time we had to ride the ski bus to the slopes. Usually we met the same skiers, mostly immigrants from Europe, on the bus. They were the only enthusiasts, who skied during those years. The bus trip was quite entertaining. We sang folk songs and told jokes. A narrow road with some very dangerous curves wound up the mountain. Two vehicles were unable to pass, except at specified areas. A bus driver had to wait until the other had passed. One of the drivers had a special talent for driving around these curves. He managed to navigate one extremely narrow curve without backing up. It was a bit scary when the back of the bus seemed to hang in the air above the steep slope. Each time this man had completed his masterpiece we applauded. Shortly before we reached the ski hut, a huge elk with gigantic antlers usually rested in the last curve beside the road watching calmly as the buses drove by.

In those early years Marmot Basin had only a single lift, a T-bar. We skied all day almost non-stop, except for a short pause at the top. It was an exhilarating feeling to look at the sun drenched, snow covered mountain peaks against the back-drop of an aquamarine-blue sky. Usually skiing one day was all that was needed to get a suntan. Exhausted we returned to our camp in the evening.

"They are showing the movie 'Cat Balloo' at the theater in Jasper," Mathew, one of Wilfried's friends, said, as we gathered around the supper table. He had noticed the announcement while driving by the previous day. "I've heard that it is very funny. Would you like to drive to Jasper to see it? There is nothing else to do here and too early to go to bed."

"But we still need to do dishes," I lamented.

"Oh, the dishes can wait! Just leave them on the table. We'll help you when we return," replied Wilfried. "Kurt, we'll use your car, it has the most room."

The movie was hilarious. We cringed with laughter until our stomachs ached. The laughter, however, subsided quickly when we stepped outside after the show. The night was pitch-black by now. Heavy snow blanketed the land. Huge flakes whirled in the air. Visibility was almost zero. Drastic changes in the weather can be anticipated in Alberta, but after the beautiful day we surely had not expected something like that. We stepped into the car, which was parked a short distance away and drove off. Kurt was at the wheel. Squeezed tightly the girls sat on the boy's knees. There were still tire tracks in the snow, but they disappeared at the town's boundaries. The road led up a steep mountain. It became more difficult to navigate. On one side rose the mountain almost vertically and on the other sloped down steeply. Despite the heavy snow flurries we opened the car's windows on both sides to assist Kurt, who drove at a snail's pace. The grass clusters at the roadside were the only markings, which we could use for orientation.

"A little bit more to the right," one called out, and then one on the other side, "now a little bit more to the left. Not so much, you must drive more to the left."

Thus we were able to return accident free to the camp. If we had slipped, we would have sailed down the steep slope. Nobody would have found us until the next day, as no other car drove that road in this terrible weather. We breathed a sigh of relief when we finally saw our tent. The dishes were buried under about two feet of snow already. We left everything on the table, and quickly crawled into our sleeping bags.

The flat tent ceiling tilted dangerously towards the middle under the heavy load of snow in the morning. We had a problem digging out of the tent. There was no sign of our dishes. We finally found them under a mountain of snow. Unwashed they were packed into a box. The tent posed a problem. It was soaking wet. Already quite heavy when dry, one could hardly lift it now. The young men had a difficult task dismantling, folding it together, and stashing it into the trunk.

After everything was stowed away, we drove to Smitty's Pancake House in Jasper for breakfast. While waiting for our meal one after the other disappeared in the washroom for morning toilette. It was such a wonderful feeling to be in a warm and dry place instead outside in the cold, wet weather.

The sun came out, and we spent another day on the slopes. Despite the cold quarters, we suffered no ill effect, but we never tried sleeping in the tent again in April. Some of the campgrounds stay open during the winter months now for the lucky owners of motor homes. The tent stood in our basement for an entire week to dry.

It was a ski trip we won't ever forget.

23. ROCK LAKE

"I won't stay here. That wind is driving me nuts," I called out. The wind almost blotted out my words.

"Then let's pack up and go home," Kurt hollered back.

The tent pegs were loosened already from the wind, so the tent came down quickly. We loaded up our camping gear and started driving.

"Can't we go somewhere else? I don't want to go home already," Andre, sitting in the back, complained.

We had driven up from Edmonton last night for a three day weekend. Rock Lake looked serene and peaceful upon arrival. There was no wind at all, and we spent an enjoyable evening sitting at the campfire and admiring the breathtaking scenery. This morning the lake was calm too until the sun peeked over the snow covered mountaintops. Suddenly the wind started to blow, whipping the lake water that the waves formed white crowns.

"I can see a path leading into the forest. It might not be so windy there," Kurt pointed to a narrow road. It was more like two ruts than a road, but driveable. "Let's see where it leads. We can always turn around if it does not get us anywhere."

We drove this path for about a mile or two when suddenly an open grassy area surrounded by high mountains and a small stream on one side appeared. Wild flowers were blooming in all colours. The wind had died down completely. It was as quiet as a cathedral without people.

Kurt stopped the motor. We all stepped out to look around.

"That is unbelievable. We are in paradise," he finally said. "Look, over there is a wooden table, a bench and a place to make a fire. We are going to stay here."

"Do you think we are allowed to do that?" I questioned.

"I can't see why not? There is no sign to say that it is private property."

"But there are no people here."

"That's all right, or are you afraid?"

"No, of course not," I replied upset about the insinuation.

Andre walked around to inspect the site. Suddenly he called out, "I've found a makeshift toilet. Come and look." A beam was nailed between two trees. A sign on one side said 'gentlemen' and one on the other 'ladies'. A large empty soup can was nailed sideways to one tree trunk with a roll of toilet paper, browned from the ravages of weather, still inside.

"I like to invite you to our new privy," Kurt laughed.

"Let's go for a walk," I suggested and everyone agreed. Turning around I noticed that the car door was still open.

"Andre, run back and close the door. We have our food inside. The smell would entice the bears and we don't want anything to happen to it."

When we opened the car door after returning from the walk, something like a grey lightning strike shot between our legs and ran quickly up a tree.

"What the dickens was that? That little monster ate all the crumbs from our cake," I called out laughing, noticing the cake, which sat on the rear window ledge completely bare of the sweet crumbs. A squirrel sat on one of the branches, watching us with its black button eyes. I had the feeling that it was laughing, having stolen the best part of the cake.

The rest of the day was spent with reading or playing ball. In the evening we ate our ready-made supper, a chicken in a can. When it started getting dark, we lit a campfire and roasted marshmallows. It was very peaceful to sit under the evening sky, watching the stars appear. At about eleven o'clock we doused the campfire, and crawled into bed. Sleep came quickly after the long walk in fresh air.

Suddenly, in the middle of the night, we were rudely awakened from a terrible noise outside the tent.

"What on earth is going on?" I whispered.

"It must be coyotes. They are fighting over the chicken bones. We should have put them away properly," Kurt replied.

The racket became louder and louder until one of the animals bumped into the tent wall that the entire construction shook violently. Our hearts were pounding. *What if the pegs don't hold?* I held on tightly to Andre, putting my arms around him. But as fast as it had started, the noise stopped.

"They must have left," Kurt said, and turned around trying to go back to sleep. I couldn't. The excitement had caused a call of nature. I knew that I wouldn't be able to wait until morning.

"I've to pee," I whispered.

"Then go. The coyotes have left."

"But I'm afraid. You must come with me and stand guard."

"O. k," he grumbled. "Let's get it over with."

We unzipped the tent flap, and crawled outside. It was pitch black. Kurt used the flashlight to shine around the tent area. In a distance of about thirty feet glowing round circles appeared, always in pairs. I thought my heart would stop beating. We realized that we were surrounded by wild animals. As fast as possible I finished my business, and then hurried back.

Bright sunshine greeted us the next morning. No signs reminded of the nightly interlude.

"Let's stay another day," Kurt suggested. We all agreed.

"I want to climb that mountain on the other side of the creek. Who wants to come along?" Kurt asked. Andre agreed, but I was tired, having been on my feet all week.

"No, you go. I'm staying here to read my book."

It was about an hour later that Kurt and Andre returned completely out of breath.

"What happened to you?" I asked concerned.

"We met a grizzly. He suddenly was there not more than ten feet away. I pushed Andre down the slope and we ran as fast as we could. When I looked back for a moment, the grizzly stood there sniffing the ground at the place we had been."

"Do you think it's safe to stay?" I asked a bit concerned.

"I guess so. We can step into the car and drive off if he shows up, but I don't think he will. Let's not panic. After all, that can happen anywhere in the wilderness of the Rockies."

The rest of the day and night were uneventful. The next day we packed our gear and started to drive home. At a muddy, sandy place we noticed many large paw prints.

"The ranger must have been here with his dogs. It's good to know that someone checks the place," Kurt casually remarked.

Shortly before arriving at Rock Lake we met the ranger. Kurt stopped, rolling down the window to greet the man.

"Hi, nice day today," he said.

"Yes, it sure is. Where are you people coming from?" the ranger inquired.

"We camped at that place beside the creek. I hope we didn't break any laws, but there was no sign to say that it is private property."

"That had to be the old Shell exploration campsite you're speaking of. No you didn't break any law. The land belongs to the Province."

"You must have been there recently with your dogs. We saw the paw prints in the soil," Kurt mentioned. The ranger started to laugh. "I don't have any dogs and I wasn't out there for years."

Kurt turned to me whispering in my ear. "It was wolves."

24. KEYS

We were tired, dead tired. Having skied all day we looked forward to dropping onto the soft car seats to drive home.

"Let's ski down one more time. We can all meet at the bus," Wilfried suggested.

"It's o.k. with me," Kurt replied, and headed down the slope. One after the other started to ski downhill. Slowly Wilfried, Andre and I arrived at the bus stop, ready to call it 'a day'. Many people were waiting there already. We stood in line.

"I wonder what has happened to Kurt. He should be here already." Wilfried remarked.

There was no sign of Kurt. Finally we saw him glide down the hill. He looked a bit dishevelled, and was covered with snow.

"Did you wipe out? You were the first one to leave," we asked.

"I sure did. I lost my keys," he replied disgruntled.

"Oh, for heaven's sake! What are we going to do? My purse with the spare keys is inside the car. Let's take another look. Perhaps we'll find them, but we'll have to go up again."

135

We took the lift up then skied down to the same place where he had fallen.

"Show me exactly where it happened," I inquired.

The snow was deep. There was a large indent from the wipe-out. We took off our skis and started to dig with our hands trying to find the keys. Daylight faded quickly, making the snow look like grey paste.

"That is useless," Kurt finally said. "We'll have to find a wire clothes hanger to pry the car door open. Maybe someone has one in their car."

We were on the last bus down to the parking lot. The temperature dropped steadily. After arriving there, we asked people if they had a hanger. Luckily one did.

Wilfried worked on the window, trying to open it a slit to release the hook. His hands became numb from the cold while doing so.

"Damn thing isn't catching," he mumbled.

"Let me try," Kurt suggested.

The parking lot was empty by the time the door finally opened, and we could get inside.

"I hope the car starts," I worried.

"The hill is quite steep, so we shouldn't have a problem. I parked it facing downhill. It can roll," Kurt commented casually.

I fished my own keys from the purse, handing them to Kurt. He tried to start the car. *Berrr, berrr, brr...r,* nothing happened. After a few more tries he gave up.

"No use killing the battery. Let's push it."

Kurt had one hand on the wheel, and then all of us started to push. Despite the steep hill, the vehicle wouldn't move. It seemed to be frozen solid. At some point it moved a few inches, then a little bit more. Darkness fell. There was no light. We pushed and pushed. Very slowly the wheels turned. It seemed a long way down. When driving this distance, it felt like a blink of an eye, but pushing the heavy car seemed to take forever. Traffic was non-existent at that time of day, as a

ll skiers had gone home or to Jasper already.

Having pushed the vehicle almost half-way down to the main highway, we noticed headlights behind us. A truck approached. Seeing our predicament, the driver stopped.

"Having a problem?" he asked grinning.

"We sure have," we replied.

"Get in the car. I will push you with the truck," he kindly offered.

Exhausted we dropped onto the seats. Our hands were icicles. We felt a slight bump when the truck made contact with our car. Then slowly the driver started to push us forward. Finally the motor caught.

What a relief! Mobile again we waved a 'thank you' to the friendly driver.

At about midnight we arrived in Edmonton, glad to be home again. A key ring is still buried on the slope at Marmot Basin, but it would not matter anymore, if someone found it. It's probably rusted by now.

25. THE LAST WORD

More than fifty years have passed since our arrival in Canada. Many changes have taken place during that time. The City of Edmonton has been transformed from a little "hick" town into a world known metropolis. People from all over the world have immigrated here. A great number have come from war ravaged countries, others fled from religious persecution or for whatever reason they had. Most have found peace and prosperity in this great country Canada and all were welcomed.

I never regretted coming to this country of ice and snow. The winters are not much different here, than they were at my home in the Giant Mountains of Silesia. Perhaps we would have achieved prosperity and peace, had we stayed in Germany, but we would have most likely never experienced the raw natural beauty of this vast country.

These crazy immigrants have become old timers, their bones are brittle and their hair has turned white. They only have a few years left to enjoy life. Looking back at those wonderful years we spent in this city of Edmonton, I must say it was the right decision we made so long ago. Of course, there were ups and downs, laughter and tears, hopes and setbacks like in any life, but for the most part we had nothing to complain. We were never hungry, thirsty or cold. Help was available when there was a need for it. The words "welcome to Edmonton" will never be forgotten. They made it easy to feel at home here. We are most fortunate living in a free society, where people are allowed to go about their business, say whatever is on their minds, and travel without restrictions or fear of being arrested or shot at, if they stay on the right path.

My memories take me back to numerous trips to the Rocky Mountains, to camping days in summer and skiing in winter. I wish I were young again, and could do it all over. I often dream of standing on top of the mountain looking down at the snow-covered winter world of Marmot Basin or Lake Louise before skiing down with the sun shining brightly from a cloudless sky. Sometimes I sit again on that little bench at Horse Shoe Lake. I look down at the still, clear waters, where huge rocks are visible below the surface. The serenity of the surrounding forest and breathtaking scenery calms my nerves. This is where heaven is on earth.

I hope my stories will inspire young people to explore the wilderness of the magnificent Rockies and experience similar adventures, as we did so many years ago. Unfortunately camping has become very expensive, almost unaffordable for the ordinary family, and ski sport is only for the rich, but there are still areas to see without spending a lot of money. Go for it. Don't wait until you are too old to enjoy.

140

Helga Tucqué

Manufactured by Amazon.ca
Bolton, ON